THE
PASTOR
AND THE PEOPLE

THE
PASTOR
AND THE PEOPLE

Building a New Partnership for Effective Ministry

Lyle E. Schaller

ABINGDON PRESS
NASHVILLE and NEW YORK

THE PASTOR AND THE PEOPLE

Copyright © 1973 by Abingdon Press

Library of Congress Cataloging in Publication Data

SCHALLER, LYLE E. The Pastor and the People.
1. Pastoral theology. 2. Theology, Practical.
I. Title.
BV4011.S33   254   72-8567

ISBN 0-687-30136-X

Portions of this book are based on material which has
been previously published. Grateful acknowledgment is
made for permission to use portions of the following:
"Picking the Pastor for the Downtown Church," by Lyle
Schaller, copyright 1970 Church Management, Inc. Reprinted by permission from the January 1970 issue of
The Clergy Journal; "What Are the Priorities?" by Lyle
Schaller. This material first appeared in the May 1972
issue of the *Christian Ministry* magazine, reprinted with
the permission of the Christian Century Foundation.

MANUFACTURED BY THE PARTHENON PRESS AT
NASHVILLE, TENNESSEE, UNITED STATES OF AMERICA

To
Walter and Harriet Ziegenhals

Contents

	Introduction	9
1.	Picking a New Pastor	16
2.	Picking a New Parish	32
3.	Pastoral Priorities	45
4.	The Interim Pastorate	56
5.	The Pastor's Compensation	65
6.	Parsonage or Housing Allowance?	72
7.	What Do You Pay Your Laymen?	80
8.	Winners and Losers	87
9.	The Quest for Quality	99
10.	Who's in Charge Here?	109
11.	Reading the Election Returns	117
12.	Assumptions in Church Finances	124
13.	Turning People Loose	133
14.	Changing the Value System	142
15.	Building Variety into the Church School	149
16.	Sunday's Eggs and the Women's Organization	159
17.	Yours or Mine?	166

Introduction

This book has been written on the assumption that individuals can learn from the experiences of other people in similar situations.

Any resemblance between the ideas, experiences, and lessons described in these pages and what has actually happened to living people is *not a coincidence.* Everything in this book is taken from what has happened in some parish or to some pastor during the past few years. The names have been changed, to repeat the familiar disclaimer, to protect the innocent, to reduce the chance of any personal embarrassment, and to eliminate the possibility that any of the persons in real life will be bothered by someone wanting to know more about a particular episode or experience. In many cases the dialogue that is presented was taken from notes made when the event described was actually occurring. Obviously, many experiences from scores of different parishes in several different denominations have been compressed together to form the one year's experience of St. John's Church and of Pastor Don Johnson.

This book is directed at three overlapping audiences.

The primary audience consists of laymen in congregations that are about to seek a new pastor, and ministers who are somewhere in that continuum, which typically extends over twelve to twenty months' time. It begins with his decision to leave the parish he is now serving, includes the period of negotiations with the next parish he will be serving and the first several months after his arrival.[1] Five of the first six chapters are directed to the laymen in the congregation seeking a new pastor and five of these first chapters are directed toward the minister moving to a new parish.

Another method of describing this primary audience is to say it includes all the persons involved in the courtship, marriage, and honeymoon period when a parish and a new pastor come together.

The second audience to which this book is directed is composed of both the laymen and the clergy in those congregations in which the honeymoon period following the arrival of the new minister is past, but where there remains an open and receptive climate for the introduction of new ideas.

The second audience is obviously the larger of these first two, and one purpose of the book is to encourage both laymen and ministers to take a fresh look at what they are doing and how they are doing it in the light of the experiences of other congregations. Sometimes the premature urge of the minister to look for greener pastures else-

---

[1] Though aware of the current concern over the use of male-oriented words and masculine pronouns in references that could and do include women, the author has chosen to use traditional terminology in this book. The decision is not to be interpreted as lacking in understanding or sympathy for women and their drive for equality and freedom; but rather as an effort to avoid the cumbersome repetition and awkward wordiness that accompany literary neutrality when the language itself provides so little of the desired neuter terminology.

where or of laymen to seek new pastoral leadership can be responded to most creatively by their working together in a re-evaluation of the work of the parish, rather than looking for a new team or seeking a new manager. Hopefully several of the chapters may provide a frame of reference for this re-evaluation.

The third audience to whom this volume is addressed should be too busy to be reading a book, but, given the world as it is, many of them do have the time and may prefer reading to traveling. This third audience is composed of local church leaders who are interested in what other congregations are doing, and who are sure that if they had the chance to go and visit other congregations they could pick up many insights and ideas that would be helpful to their parish.

They are absolutely correct in this basic assumption. There is much that local church leaders can learn from visiting other parishes and talking with the people there. Such a procedure is far superior to reading a book. However, not every parish leader who believes this has the opportunity to visit other churches. Thus those who cannot get out and see firsthand what is happening in other churches constitute the third audience for this book.

For the past dozen years I have had the enviable opportunity of visiting from two to three hundred congregations annually. Some of these visits are for only an hour or two; most are for a day or two; and a few, for four or five or six days.

The material in this book is drawn from those experiences with congregations representing two dozen denominations and religious bodies in all parts of the United States. Out of these experiences have come the incidents, ideas, insights, lessons, and illustrations that are recounted in the following pages.

The first chapter is drawn from the experience of working with a number of pulpit or call or pastor-parish relations committees, and from the observations of denominational executives who are responsible for pastoral placement. The basic intent of this chapter is to suggest the idea of developing a systematic agenda of concerns that will help the lay leadership in a parish as they participate in the process of selecting a new pastor. The use of such a systematic approach will tend to bring to the surface those subjects which either the parish leaders or the prospective pastor believe are "nonnegotiable." The earlier these are identified, the better for everyone concerned.

The second chapter looks at the same process, but from the perspective of a prospective new pastor, while the third chapter suggests a procedure for surfacing and discussing the varying points of view about the priorities on the new minister's time and talent.

One of the most neglected concepts in the pastoral placement process is the occasional need for an interim pastor to bridge the transition between what was and what is yet to come in a parish. Some of the situations in which an interim pastorate may be advisable are identified in the fourth chapter.

The fifth and sixth chapters review four dimensions of the "compensation package." The most obvious of the four is the economic compensation. The other three are satisfactions, expectations, and housing.

The subject of satisfactions, or psychi rewards, is important to many laymen as well as to clergymen and that is discussed in the seventh chapter. This chapter also marks the beginning of the second section of this volume which is concerned with the practice of ministry after the new pastor has arrived.

Every pastor has the choice of learning from his own experiences and relying on the passage of time to build up his inventory of skills gained from experience, or of exploiting the experiences of others to build up his skills at a faster pace. The eighth chapter should be of interest to those who prefer the second of these alternatives and seek to profit from the experiences of others.

One of the most significant trends of this era that will have a major impact on the parish in the 1970s is the new emphasis on quality. Some of the implications of this trend are discussed in chapter 9.

It is easy to oversimplify the decision-making processes in the parish, and the next two chapters offer two different approaches that may be helpful in gaining a clearer understanding of how others view what is happening. The process described in chapter 10 has been used in several dozen congregations and invariably has provided material for productive discussion on the various influences on the decision-making process in that congregation.

In the next chapter several assumptions are suggested about church finances that may arouse considerable disagreement from some readers. They are based on the assumption that the churches have been more effective in teaching stewardship than in developing effective internal communications systems.

The last three chapters present some ideas and practices that are being used today to increase the attractiveness and effectiveness of the church school, to revitalize the women's organization in the parish, and to broaden the base of ownership of goals in the parish.

For those readers with a strong interest in local church planning, or for those who want the author to explain what he perceives as his own bias, this book can be viewed as the third of a three-volume series. In the first volume, *The Local Church Looks to the Future*, the emphasis was on defining purpose, formulating goals, developing strategy, and responding to a series of specific questions such as building programs, interchurch cooperation, self-evaluation, and evangelism.

The second volume in this series, *Parish Planning*, emphasized a pragmatic approach to the implementation of goals and getting things done in the parish.

This volume looks at the subject of local church planning from the perspective of building a team in which the pastor and the laymen work together in ministry. The assumption here is that the minister should be *one* of the leaders in the parish, but as a professional he has certain responsibilities, not only as the theologian in residence and the conservator of the orthodox faith, but also as an innovator and as a consultant to his own congregation on process.

This model or style of ministerial leadership is not exceptionally rare. I am greatly indebted to the many very effective pastors who have, by their actions more than by their words, helped me conceptualize this style of ministerial leadership. A sympathetic view of this style of ministerial leadership is one of the more obvious biases that runs through this volume.

Ideally this introduction should include a list of the scores of exceptionally able, remarkably dedicated, and unusually creative pastors and laymen from whom so much has been "borrowed" for this volume. There are two reasons for not doing this. The more obvious is the lack of space. The second is an inadequate note-taking system which guarantees that the publication of such a list would also produce some embarrassing omissions. It is easier and safer simply to say to all who have contributed to the contents of this volume, "Thank you!"

This book is dedicated to a pastor and his wife who have served as a model of ministry, who have displayed a remarkable appreciation of the worshiping congregation and who have contributed much to the writing of this book.

1

Picking a New Pastor

"If you ask me, I believe we should look for a man who is in his thirties," suggested Jack Peterson. "If we can find a young minister maybe we can reach some of the young couples in the community who don't like to go to any church."

"Normally I would be inclined to agree with you," replied Betty White, "but I think, in our situation, the number one requirement is for a pastor who has the ability to bring people together and to help a congregation function as a unified organization."

"Those are important characteristics," commented the man who later was to become the chairman of this committee at St. John's, "but I think we need a man who can be a leader, who can give direction to this parish, and who can help us move ahead."

"You're talking about a leadership style that can be pretty authoritarian at times," interjected Everett Wright. "I was talking to Paul Peters from the denominational headquarters the other day, and he commented on a remarkable similarity between the attitudes and practices of the minister fresh out of seminary and the pastor who is only a few years from retirement. In both cases, according to Dr. Peters, each man has his own agenda and doggedly sticks to it, regardless of the desires or needs of the congregation. Now I hear some of you saying that we should look for a pastor who, regardless of his age, comes in with his own agenda and forces it on us. I can't support that. I think we need a man who is able and willing to help us develop an agenda based on the needs of this congregation and to work from that agenda, not one he brings with him."

"Now wait a minute, Everett," responded the advocate of strong leadership, "we're not so far apart. You're saying what I was trying to say. We need someone who can give leadership and help get this parish moving. We're stuck on dead center. Church attendance is going down, our income has just about leveled off, interest in the church is dropping fast, the Sunday school is sick, the women's organization is dying, the men's club is dead. That's our agenda!"

"You've just described some of the reasons Pastor Case decided to move to another church," replied Jack Peterson. "Do you think we should expect that simply getting a new pastor will solve all those problems?"

"I don't expect him to solve them all by himself without any help," said the advocate of strong leadership, "but I firmly believe our pastor should be able to help us identify our problems, figure out the causes, and lead us in solving them. In baseball the losing team gets a new manager. St. John's is a losing team today. We need a new manager!"

"I read a good definition of an attractive style of leadership," interjected Betty White. "Robert K. Greenleaf says

17

that the key element in a servant style of leadership is foresight. He says a leader should be able to look beyond today and see the probable consequences of each alternative course of action.[1] I think that's what we need here, someone who can be a part of a leadership team in this parish and yet, at the same time, have a kind of detachment that lets him look at what we're doing with a more critical eye than any of us can bring to the situation."

As the members of St. John's Church continued to talk about a replacement for their pastor, who had announced his resignation, it became increasingly obvious that what they were seeking was a set of guidelines they could use in picking the next pastor.

Perhaps a better way to approach this subject is to think in terms of a common agenda that can be helpful to all parties in this process. These include the representatives from the parish, the regional denominational executive responsible for pastoral placement, and the prospective pastors or candidates.

Each one of these three parties has his own private agenda. For the parish leaders it may be getting the best minister available; it may be a deliberate decision to look for someone who can pour oil on troubled waters; it may be the hope that the new pastor will solve all their problems by himself; or it may be simply to find the best person available for the least amount of money.

The denominational executive in the regional judicatory usually has several vacancies to worry about and an even larger number of ministers wanting to move. In one case he may find himself giving large quantities of time and energy in an effort to find the "right" minister for a vacant

[1] Robert K. Greenleaf, "The Servant As Leader, *Journal of Current Social Issues*, Spring, 1971, pp. 4-29.

pulpit at a crucial point in that congregation's history. In another, he may find himself trying to fit a square peg in a round hole—and hoping it will not pop out for a year or two, until he has more time to give to that parish. In another case, he may conclude that the parish, after a succession of three outstanding pastors, has an obligation to take a minister who is more lovable than competent or who is neither competent nor lovable, but needs to leave where he is now.

The third party in these negotiations, although from his own perspective he may see himself as the first party, is the prospective new pastor. His agenda may be dominated by a desire to find a parish that fully challenges his capabilities or by a very strong desire to leave where he is or by the desire to move to a different section of the country or by the need for an increase in his compensation or by the longing for a different type of parish than he has been serving or by a desire to serve "one more church" before retirement.

All too often these three parties discuss the selection of the next pastor for a parish without the aid of a common agenda. Each tends to wait more or less patiently until he can get his own agenda on the top of the stack and does not give adequate attention to the items which should be on all three agendas, but may not be on any of them.

It may be more effective to develop a basic common agenda for all three parties to use as a beginning point in the discussions.

The following list is suggested not as a universal agenda that can be used in all situations, but rather as a checklist or a supplementary agenda to be used in addition to the lists each party brings to the discussions.

1. The item that should be at the top of the agenda is *purposes*. What is the purpose of this congregation, meeting at this geographical location at this point in history? What do the members believe the Lord is calling their parish to do and to be? All parties should be prepared and willing to discuss purpose in terms of function, program, mission, and role, as well as in traditional theological clichés.

If the pulpit committee does not bring up this matter, or if they fumble when the prospective candidate raises questions about purpose, he would be well advised to pursue the subject vigorously. It may turn out that if he accepts a call, his first task will be to help the congregation review and redefine this question of purpose and role.

On the other hand, the pulpit committee should be wary of any prospective candidate who does not raise questions about how this parish defines its purpose and explains its reason for being.

2. Program is important but it is of secondary importance. "Form follows function" is an expression used frequently by architects. Churchmen should recognize that similarly program is an outgrowth of purpose.

If, in the inevitable discussion on the program of the church, all the conversation by the pulpit committee is directed to the content of the program and to the importance of "making it go," the pastor should push the committees to describe how the program relates to purpose.

The pulpit committee should expect to be asked these questions. If they do not hear them they should inquire how the pastor sees this relationship between purpose and program.

3. All parties should present a strong orientation to the future. This is extremely important in the case of certain

types of churches. If the pulpit committee appears to be out to recruit a minister who has the determination and ability to turn the clock back to 1927 or 1949, the prospective candidate may find this to be a good time to terminate the interview.

Likewise, if the minister being interviewed turns out to have a strong orientation to yesterday, the pulpit committee probably should make the interview as brief as possible. This may be the kind of minister the committee members want, but it almost certainly is not the kind of pastor this church will need in the 1970s.

4. An openness to change, creativity, and innovation is another item that each party should look for in the other.

Unless this characteristic is present in *both* the new pastor and the leadership of the congregation, it may mean the wasting of the unique opportunities for innovation that are present during the "honeymoon period" that usually accompanies the coming of a new pastor. In most parishes a new pastor usually should and will spend the honeymoon period getting acquainted and building up a feeling of mutual trust before becoming involved in proposals for change. In today's church there may not be time for that luxury. That first year may turn out to be the best—and occasionally the last—opportunity for creative innovation.

5. The present *and future clientele* should be on both agendas. Before seeking a new pastor the congregation should take a very careful look at its membership and constituency, both present and potential. Too often this is not done. The pulpit committee offers a description of, and the prospective pastor bases his response on, a stereotyped impression of the clientele that may corre-

21

spond more to the past than to the present and bears little relationship to the future.

Three current trends can be cited to illustrate this point. In many communities a large proportion of the present membership of the parish may be composed of mature women without husbands—widows, spinsters, and divorcées. In one church 40 percent of the members are single adult women. In another, the new pastor was amazed to discover that 17 of the 22 members of his congregation who died during the first year of his pastorate were in this category.

What does this say about the future? First, the spinster is disappearing from American society. While it is still true that in countries such as Ireland, France, and Italy 20 to 45 percent of the female population never marry, this is not the trend in the United States. Here the trend is in the other direction. In 1940, 81 percent of all women in the 35-44 age group had married. In 1970 this figure had jumped to 94 percent. Second, while the number of widowed women has nearly doubled since 1940 (and the number of widowed men has declined slightly), there is a strong national trend for these widowed women to move out of the central city and into the suburbs. One reason for this is that a rapidly increasing percentage of widows, due to Social Security and other pension systems, are in comfortable economic circumstances and can afford a wider choice in housing.

A second trend is that today the in-migration to the central part of the city consists largely of young adults, poor people, and black people.

A third trend is the current sharp increase in crime and violence in the downtown area. This has encouraged many of the residents who otherwise would have remained in the central part of the city to move to what they expect will be a safer neighborhood, and this has accelerated an already rapid migration out of the central city.

This means that in terms of a neighborhoood constituency some churches, who yesterday were directing a large share of their ministry to older white women, tomorrow (or today?) will be challenged to minister in a neighborhood occupied largely by alienated blacks, the angry poor, and unattached young people.

On the other hand, it should also be recognized that the second fastest growing population group in the United States is widowed women age fifty and over. For thousands of congregations this may be the number one opportunity to enlarge their ministry.

6. One of the most significant changes occurring in many churches is a shift in emphasis from professionalism to participation. This can be seen in the development of a volunteer choir to replace the paid choir, in the disappearance of the pastor who "ran the church," and in more widespread participation by laymen in functions that once were the responsibility of paid staff members.

There is still nothing resembling a consensus on this point among either laymen or clergymen. Therefore it is extremely important that there be a frank exchange of views and values on this question. Is the congregation seeking a person who will be their leader and see that every function of the church is carried out with professional skill and finesse? Or is the congregation looking for an enabler, who will help them carry out their ministry? (See chapter 3 for one means of discovering the expectations of people on this point.)

7. Nearly every pulpit committee is interested in the

competence of a prospective candidate as a preacher. Not infrequently this is the first item on their agenda.

While preaching is important, and it is far more important than many pastors are willing to admit, the pulpit committee would do well to enlarge this item on their agenda to the larger subject of corporate worship. How competent is this minister as a leader of worship? What is his attitude on the number of worship services that should be held each week? Is he primarily interested in one large crowd each Sunday morning, or is he open to scheduling two or three or four services each Sunday in order to increase the total number of people who will share in the worship experience? Is he open to innovation and variety in worship?

The minister who is considering a call to a church also should be asking these and similar questions of the pulpit committee. What is expected of him in his role as a worship leader? Do these expectations coincide with what appears to be the contemporary need?

8. A subject rarely explored adequately in these discussions is the length of the pastorate of the man who is being replaced. If the new man is following a pastor who served the church for two decades or more, the chances are four out of five that he will encounter problems that may greatly shorten his tenure.

While the exceptions to this generalization merit acknowledgment, approximately four-fifths of the pastors who serve the same congregation for over twenty years leave a legacy which greatly handicaps their successors. This legacy often includes a limited capacity of the congregation to adapt to change and the repeated references to how "Dr. Jones did that" or how "Dr. Smith always did this." This legacy also often involves a loyalty to the beloved pastor rather than to Christ and his church, an orientation to the past rather than to the present, and, most serious of all, a definition of purpose that has increasingly emphasized survival and a ministry to the members. This legacy often includes a growing neglect of evangelism, prophetic witness, and involvement in mission in the community.

Here again is a subject that should be on both agendas, and frank discussion should be encouraged. (See chapter 4 for an elaboration of this very important point.)

9. The selection of a new pastor should be accompanied by a review of the compensation of the minister. One part of this package that may be overlooked is the sabbatical leave for study or travel, or simply for rest and rehabilitation. A growing number of churches are including a sabbatical as a part of the agreement in calling a new minister.

A few are going beyond this and providing unusual opportunities for the professional growth of the pastor. (See chapter 5 for an extended discussion on this subject.)

10. Who are the neighboring churches? What are they doing? What is the extent of interchurch cooperation with other parishes?

If the pulpit committee does not have this subject on its agenda, the prospective candidate should bring it up. In a very few minutes he can learn a lot about the perspective of the pulpit committee by asking a few questions about what the other parishes in the area are doing.

One of the interesting recent products of the ecumenical movement is that occasionally a pulpit committee will invite the pastor of a nearby parish to serve as a nonvoting observer as they interview candidates.

11. One of the most vital issues in the life of nearly every congregation is the necessity of maintaining a sense of unity and common purpose among people who represent a wide range of views, and who come from widely differing backgrounds. The issue of unity in diversity should be on the common agenda. Which is given the higher priority by the various parties to the discussion, unity or diversity?

This tends to be a greater problem for the downtown church than for any other type parish because of the greater differences among the members in age, income, education, social and economic views, political affiliation, denominational background, racial, ethnic, or subcultural identification, definitions of the role of purpose of the downtown church, and length of membership. In most cities the downtown church either does include, *or has the potential* for including, in its constituency an extraordinarily wide range of people who together approach being a cross section of the community.

In some congregations the potential divisiveness of these differences is overcome by a strong doctrinal unity. In a few it is overcome by a remarkable sense of discipline, growing out of a strong commitment to Christ—although this is exceedingly rare in a large parish.

The most common approach to this problem is for the congregation to become a collection of groups rather than a collection of individuals. Each group has to have a sense of its own identity and purpose and also must respect and tolerate the identity and purpose of the other groups. This concept of pluralism within the parish is a very important consideration when one discusses the future of any parish. Therefore, this entire issue should be on the agenda of both the pulpit committee and the prospective candidate.

12. Closely related to this is the matter of visiting. Too many congregations are looking for a pastor with only two qualifications: competence as a preacher and a willingness to call in the home. While both are important, the pulpit committee of most parishes which have these two items at the very top of their lists probably is helping to destroy the parish it represents.

This is especially true of the parish with 1,200 or more members. In a congregation of that size the issue of dealing with diversity will be a major challenge to the pastor. This and other responsibilities will leave him little time for calling. An associate will have to do most of the routine calling. A pastor of a 3,000-member parish in Texas responded to this subject by describing his own role, as he said, "When you are the pastor of a congregation as big as this one, you're not a shepherd, you're a rancher."

13. To be an effective pastor in the 1970s means hard work and lots of it! The minister should have the emotional security, the administrative skill, and the experience that enable him to delegate responsibility, but he also must be a hard worker himself. Most effective pastors share one common characteristic; each is a remarkably hard worker.

There is one major exception to this generalization. This is the small and long-established parish; typically it averages 60 to 100 at worship on Sunday morning, and has a full-time pastor. In many of these parishes the hardworking, hard-driving, and efficient pastor can be a very destructive force. He can destroy both the parish and himself by trying to make what should be regarded as a part-time job into a full-time vocation, by trying to make a small congregation "perform" like the 600-member congregation served by his old seminary roommate, and by trying to develop a response that quantitatively far exceeds the resources available in that parish.

In these parishes the most effective pastors usually are those who know how to channel their discretionary time left over after "paying the rent"[2] into serving as a volunteer in community, denominational, or interdenominational functions, and/or into golfing, fishing, and spending more time with the family.

14. The second most important characteristic that the pulpit committee should be looking for as they seek a new pastor is a candidate's attitude toward people. Does he have a deep love for people? Is he sufficiently secure himself, both emotionally and spiritually, that he neither threatens nor is threatened by people? Does this concern for people come through? Do others find it easy to relate to him, to trust him, and to have confidence in him?

In the past many churches have not placed much emphasis on this point in selecting a pastor. Frequently they sought a man who could build and maintain the institution, and they called a minister who was object-oriented rather than person-centered in his world view.

Today and tomorrow the primary responsibility of the church will be a ministry to people, both individually and in groups. Frequently this will be in a pastoral role to an individual or a family at a time of misfortune or disaster. At other times it will be in a prophetic role as a leader in an unpopular cause. Occasionally it will be in the minister's role as an enabler, helping others to discover and fulfill their ministry. Regularly it will be in his role as an administrator,

[2] This reference to "paying the rent" is from James D. Glasse, *Putting It Together in the Parish* (Nashville: Abingdon Press, 1972), pp. 53-61.

as he relates to both the paid staff and the volunteer leaders of the parish. In these and other roles the most important quality a pastor can bring to his task is a love for people, an interest in their problems, and a concern for them as God's children.

15. Finally, and while it must be last, the most important of all the items on this common agenda is the question of whether the potential new minister feels the Lord is calling him to this church. To some this may seem so obvious that it barely rates mention. Experience, however, suggests this point cannot be overemphasized. Too often the pulpit committee concludes they have found the man they have been seeking and begin to pressure him to accept. Too often the minister is so determined to leave his present pastorate that in fact he is really looking for a new job rather than seeking a call.

While it is difficult, and perhaps pointless, to attempt to elaborate on this subject, let it be said simply that unless the pulpit committee believes the candidate "sees the vision" they should keep looking. If they extend a call, the candidate would be well advised to reject it unless he does "see the vision"!

Little or nothing has been said here about salary, housing, the prospective candidate's family, administrative ability, competence as a counselor or fund raiser, or experience as a community leader. These omissions were deliberate, but should not be misconstrued as suggesting that these are unimportant considerations. This list was intended only to supplement the agendas of the two parties and to bring to their attention items one or both might overlook. It is not offered as a complete list, only as a supplement to the agenda of each party involved in the extremely important responsibility of picking a pastor for a particular parish.

There are a few subjects which some readers may feel are major omissions. These include the pastor's total compensation, the issue of a housing allowance versus a church-owned parsonage, the varying expectations on the new pastor's time and talent, the age of the prospective pastor, and the role of the pastor's spouse in the parish. The first three of these are discussed in subsequent chapters. The last two merit a brief mention here.

Many congregations display great concern about the prospective pastor's spouse. They may be concerned over the spouse's education, employment, interest in functioning as an active leader in the congregation, talents as a gracious host/hostess, or role in denominational affairs. At best these are of second-level importance. The only two important questions for a congregation to raise about the prospective pastor's spouse are these: First, is the spouse happy that his/her mate is a pastor? If the spouse is unhappy with the mate's vocation as a pastor this merits consideration. Second, is the spouse happy with the role as the spouse of a pastor and all that may imply? This issue will grow in importance with the sharp increase in female pastors during the 1970s.

The growing pattern of the wife having employment outside the home and the increasing number of women in the professional ministry mean that these are two very important questions, regardless of whether the prospective pastor is a man or a woman.

A few years ago a joke circulating in one of the Presbyterian denominations noted that at age forty-three a person was old enough to be elected President of the United States and young enough to be voted the most valuable player in the American Football League; but at forty-three a minister was too old to expect a call from a Presbyterian congregation. The references to the careers of John F. Kennedy and George Blanda do contrast with the value systems of many parish leaders who voted for the former and applauded the last-minute heroics of the latter, but who also are convinced that "our next pastor should be under forty."

Rather than relying on chronological age, local church leaders might find it more helpful to ask another series of questions when interviewing a prospective pastor. Of more value than emphasizing his age might be the answers to questions such as these: "What did you learn during the last year that will make you a more effective pastor this coming year?" "How do you believe your experience where you are now would be of help to you if you came here as the pastor of this congregation?" "What were the most helpful books that you read during the past year?" "What would you like to be doing ten years from now?" "What are your expectations for the future of the parish?"

As parish leaders listen to the responses to these questions, they may conclude there is a vast difference between the person who has had fifteen years of experience and the individual who has had one year of experience fifteen times. That distinction may be a more useful index than chronological age in picking a new pastor.

2

Picking a New Parish

"We had just bought a new car, being careful to get one that would fit in that short garage at Trinity's parsonage, and we had absolutely no plans to move when the call came asking if we would be interested in going to St. John's," explained Donald Johnson, the thirty-seven-year-old minister at Trinity Church, who was in his fifth year as the pastor of that congregation.

"My first response was to say I wasn't interested; but after we talked a little longer I finally agreed to meet with their committee next Thursday evening. Now that I have agreed to talk to them, I'm not sure what to say. Do you have any suggestions?"

There are at least five parts in an adequate answer to Pastor Johnson's question. Perhaps the best place to begin is with the first interview, which is the next item on his schedule.

When a pastor goes to meet with the pulpit or pastor-parish relations or screening committee from another parish, he immediately faces a very basic question. Is he going with the expectation that the committee will interview him or with the expectation that he will interview the committee? Or is he going without an agenda or plan of his own and thinking of the meeting as a blank slate and hoping that someone will pick up the chalk and begin to write?

A pastor, such as Mr. Johnson, who was not planning on moving or who does not have to move, has a comparatively large degree of freedom in planning for the interview, but freedom does not grant him the right to be irresponsible.

A reasonable expectation is that the pastor is entitled to use one half of that first evening in interviewing the committee. If he is prepared to assume the role of the interviewer for an hour to an hour and a half, he probably can make this a much more productive evening for both the committee and himself.

It is not unusual for the committee to consist of from seven to twelve persons. Therefore, it is advantageous for all if the pastor asks permission to open the discussion with a few general questions. By doing this he can ensure that every person present has at least two or three opportunities to speak early in the evening. This tends to encourage some who might otherwise be silent all evening to feel a greater degree of freedom to speak. If the pastor encourages or allows the committee to ask questions of him for an hour or longer before he raises any questions of the committee members, he may be encouraging a situation in which he and the chairman will do 70 percent of the talking. Chances are, the other 30 percent will be divided among four or five members of the committee and the remaining committee members will be shut out.

After the preliminaries have been completed Mr. Johnson might say something like this, "I know you have many questions you want to ask me, but it might help me to respond to your questions more intelligently if you would permit me to ask a couple of questions first." If he receives a favorable signal he might follow with, "First, it certainly would help me if each one of you would tell me individually why you are a member of St. John's Church. What were the circumstances, the event or the person or the reason that accounts for your being a member of St. John's today rather than of some other congregation?"

With this question Don, in the space of ten or fifteen minutes, is able to (1) give every member of the committee a chance to be heard; (2) learn something about each committee member as a person; (3) identify both the timid and the bold persons on the committee; (4) discover a little about some of the major characteristics of St. John's; (5) determine the "mix" of the people that constitute the committee; (6) reveal to some degree how and why people join St. John's; and (7) help the committee members discover some things about each other and about St. John's that were unknown to some.

Following this initial round, Pastor Johnson may want to raise a second question to which each committee member again is asked to respond individually. The following questions have proved to be helpful in this process in other congregations. The prospective candidate may want to pick one or two from this list and adapt them, or he may prefer to develop his own.

"What is the most important strength or asset of St. John's as a church?"

"In terms of ministry and program what do you folks at St. John's do best?"

"What new ministries or programs have been added recently or are under consideration?"

"If you could change one thing at St. John's, what would it be?"

"If you could wave a magic wand and have one wish about the life, program, and ministry of this parish come true, what would be your wish?"

"If you could change *one* thing in all that we do together as a denomination, what would you change?"

"If a twenty-nine-year-old teacher, his wife, and their two children, ages five and three, moved to your community from Seattle next month and visited St. John's on their own initiative, why might they decide to join? Why might they look elsewhere for a new church home?"

"If one of your members died and left St. John's $50,000 in her will with absolutely no restrictions on the use of the money, how do you think people would decide the money should be used?"

"What were the major goals that you as a congregation set for yourselves this year and how are you doing in reaching these?"

"When was St. John's at its peak in strength and vitality?"

Rarely will it be possible for the pastor to ask more than two or three of these subjective questions, but often asking even two of them not only will help free everyone to participate in the subsequent discussion, but also will elicit verbal and nonverbal responses that can be very enlightening to the pastor—and often to some of the committee members!

Why?

Sooner or later, if it appears that Don Johnson and the people from St. John's are interested in pursuing the conversations, the time will come when Don will want to review some of the statistical data about St. John's. How many people are members of this congregation? What is the average attendance at worship? How large is the church school? What were the total receipts last year?

A review of these data often can be more helpful if they are examined in a frame of reference consisting of these four elements.

1. What are the most useful statistics?

2. What are the trends over several years?

3. How do these figures compare with those of similar type congregations?

4. If these numbers show significant changes from year to year, or contrast sharply with those of similar type congregations, why is this the case here at St. John's?

Perhaps the most significant single figure that can be used to describe a congregation to an outsider, and certainly the best single index to use in predicting other characteristics or trends, is the average attendance at worship on Sunday morning. There are a few congregations in which the qualifying phrase "on Sunday morning" will produce a distorted response because of the tradition of Sunday afternoon or Sunday evening worship, or because of a recent shift to a major service of corporate worship on Thursday evening for those who will be away over the weekend. In perhaps 97 percent of the congregations in American Protestantism, however, the key index is still the number of people present for worship on Sunday morning.

This number can be compared to the communicant membership figure, to the average worship attendance for the past several years, to the worship attendance of similar type and size congregations, and to the receipts from the membership.

It may be helpful to follow the Reverend Mr. Johnson as he reviewed the statistical data at St. John's and look at a few of the occasions when he felt constrained to ask the committee "why?"

St. John's reports a confirmed membership of 540, and that figure has hovered between 525 and 575 since seven years ago when it dropped from 683. Why?

"That really is a deceptive change," replied one of the committee members very easily. "The year after Pastor Case came—he is the minister who is now leaving us for another pastorate—we decided to clean the rolls. The membership rolls had been neglected for years and it turned out we were paying denominational apportionments on 127 people who were dead, long-gone from the community, or had simply lost interest in being a part of our church. I guess the previous pastor felt the denomination needed the money from these assessments or that it helped the prestige of the parish to report the larger figure."

For the previous six years the worship attendance at St. John's had averaged 226, 221, 219, 223, 213, and 199.

Why did it drop 10 percent in two years after being on a plateau for four years?

"Well, we're not sure," replied the chairman of the committee from St. John's, "but Pastor Case explained that this decline was one of the reasons he felt that he should leave for another pastorate at this point in history. Frankly, I for one agree it was time for him to move on. We had two major internal differences of opinion and a number of people had been offended. One was over the new plans for confirmation and the other, the music used

37

in the worship service. Some feelings were hurt and little was done by anyone to be more considerate of the reactions of others!"

As he looked at these two sets of figures Pastor Johnson concluded that an attendance at worship equal to 40 percent of the membership was typical for a parish of this size and type in his denomination. If, however, this had been a denomination where that ratio is higher, such as the American Lutheran Church, he would have pushed further in his questioning. In the ALC, for example, a parish with a confirmed membership of 540 could be expected to average 250 to 350 at worship rather than 220.

The receipts for the previous year at St. John's had been $51,300, or an average of $256 per average attender at worship. Since St. John's is a stable parish in a stable suburban community, Pastor Johnson had expected this figure to be approximately $250, and therefore he said nothing about it. If this had been a small rural congregation he would have expected the annual receipts to be $150 times the average attendance; if it had been a 1,200-member, downtown, "First Church" type he would have expected the giving level to be in the range of $300 to $400 per average attender; while in the 1,900-member, metropolitan type church he would have expected it to be between $400 and $500.

When he saw that the total receipts for the past six years had gone from $41,200 to $45,000 to $48,400 to $51,600 to $52,080 to $51,300, he asked two questions.

"Why did the total receipts increase 25 percent in three years?"

"Why did receipts level off during the past two years?"

Pastor Johnson next looked at what, in many congregations, is the second most useful statistical index: the number of persons who transferred their membership by letter into St. John's, minus the number who transferred out. He came out with this set of figures for the previous six years: 21, 19, 12, 2, −9, −27. With a trace of anxiety in his voice he asked two questions.

"Why has there been this change from a net gain of 21 by transfer in to a net loss of 27 by transfers out?"

"Why has it been a consistent downward curve year after year for six years?"

Don was especially concerned about this series of figures because he thought it might reflect the changing reactions of newcomers to the community and of visitors to St. John's to what they found or saw there. In responding to his first two questions on this subject the people from St. John's emphasized the mobility of people today, adding that in the past couple of years some unhappy members had transferred to other churches in the community. While he listened Pastor Johnson formulated another question on this subject.

"Am I hearing you say that six years ago newcomers to the community found St. John's to be an attractive parish when they went church shopping, but today, either they don't even shop St. John's, or if they do they decide to keep looking?"

Next Don noted that membership losses by death had been 9, 4, 8, 9, 8, and 10 for the past six years, or an average of 8 per year. In that denomination the annual death rate is 12 per 1,000 confirmed members. The rate at St. John's was an average of 15 per 1,000 members per year.

"Why," he asked the committee, "is the death rate so high in this twenty-two-year-old suburban parish? I would have guessed the death rate would be only about half of what it is."

"Well, it's true that this congregation is less than twenty-five years old," was the reply. "But, in case you didn't know, perhaps a fourth of our members are from the old St. Mark's Church, a congregation of older people in the inner city that merged with our church back in 1959. I suspect that may be one reason for what you suggest is an unusually high death rate."

"I also have a question about the relationship between confirmations and deaths. You said earlier that at St. John's young people are received into confirmed membership when they are fourteen. There are about 4.2 million people celebrating their fourteenth birthday each year, and less than 2 million dying each year in this country," continued Don, reviewing St. John's statistical record.

"Yet for the last six years you report 48 deaths and only 81 confirmations for all ages. I would have expected that in a suburban community such as yours you would be averaging far more than twice as many confirmations each year as losses by death. Why is this total confirmation figure only 81 rather than somewhere in the neighborhood of 100 to 150?

"Please don't misunderstand the point of my questions," he added, when he suddenly realized that some members of the committee from St. John's felt that he was either criticizing or attacking them.

"We're here to talk about the possibility of my coming to serve as your pastor at St. John's. We met once and talked in generalities. You've heard me preach; and now we're meeting again to talk specifics," he continued. "I came to this meeting after doing my homework, and I simply am trying to learn about your parish and what makes it tick. I'm not trying to be judgmental, I'm simply trying to learn enough that I can ask the kind of questions that will help all of us come to the right decision."

Later that same evening they began to talk gingerly about salary. The committee members were surprised to discover that Don's salary as pastor of the 390-member Trinity congregation was $8,400, or $200 above what St. John's had been paying Pastor Case.

"We had been warned that when we went out to look for a new pastor we would have to expect to pay close to $9,000," conceded the chairman of the committee from St. John's. "I must confess that I didn't realize that we were as far behind other parishes in what we are paying as we seem to be. However, don't worry about salary. We'll take care of you if we agree you're the minister for St. John's."

"I'm not worried about what my salary might be if I come to St. John's," quickly replied Pastor Johnson. "My question is why did St. John's fall behind other comparable parishes in what they have been paying in recent years? The six-year record shows the salary went from $6,200 to $6,600 to $7,100 to $7,600 to $8,000 to the current $8,200. Why has there been a dropping off in the rate of the annual increase? That's the point that interests me now!"

What's the Type?

In these negotiations with St. John's Church, Pastor Johnson moved from the question of a strategy for that first interview to a series of "why" type questions growing out of the statistical data that had been made available to him.

A third area that merits exploration by the minister who is contemplating a move to a new parish is the type or style of parish under consideration.

In this case the move Pastor Johnson was contemplating involved at least three types of change. The most obvious was a change from the one-hundred-year-old, 390-member Trinity Church, in a stable Iowa county seat community with 5,000 residents, to a younger but larger congregation in a growing suburban community in a metropolitan area with close to a million residents.

Less obvious but equally significant would be the change in Pastor Johnson's personal and professional relationships as he moved from a rural to a highly urbanized community.

The most subtle change, however, would be in moving from a firmly established and stable county-seat-town type parish to a congregation which gave several signs of being in the process of changing from one type of parish to another.[1] The data that have been mentioned earlier suggest that St. John's may be experiencing what some church leaders describe as "a change of life." For more than a decade St. John's had resembled the typical young and growing suburban parish. When it passed the 600 mark in confirmed members, many people assumed that was but another milepost on a growth curve that would bring St. John's to the 1,000-member mark by its twenty-fifth birthday. Along about its fifteenth year, however, the growth curve began to level off, and St. John's, after a

[1] For a more extended discussion of the question of types of churches and for detailed descriptions of several different types of congregations see Lyle E. Schaller, *Parish Planning* (Nashville: Abingdon Press, 1971), pp. 162-210.

vigorous pruning of the membership roll, began to show signs that it was leveling off on a rather comfortable plateau. More recently it began to appear that this plateau was no longer level, but was beginning to tilt downward at one end.

A few members of the committee felt uneasy about recent trends, and some of the questions Pastor Johnson had been asking had increased their uneasiness about the situation at St. John's. All the members were completely convinced, however, that everything would be all right again if only they could find the right pastor.

They were completely unprepared for Pastor Johnson's next question, however.

"I think I know the type of parish I am in back at Trinity," said Don in introducing his question, "but I am still uncertain what type of church you have at St. John's. I know Trinity, I know what it is, I know what is expected of me there, and I have a reasonable level of confidence that my gifts and skills are adequate for what is required of a pastor in that situation.

"I still don't know what type of church St. John's is," he continued. "I don't know what gifts and skills are required of a pastor in a parish such as St. John's is today or will be tomorrow, and therefore I honestly don't know whether I am the person you are looking for or not."

It would be unrealistic to expect the committee from St. John's to respond immediately with a thorough and analytical answer to a question such as Don had just asked. It also would be less than wise for Don to overlook the critical importance of this question. To move from Trinity to St. John's would be a far different type of change than to move from Trinity to a five-hundred-member congregation in another midwestern county seat town.

What Are Your Expectations?

By opening up the question of the type of parish St. John's was, Pastor Johnson did accomplish two things. First, he helped everyone involved in the discussions, including himself, to begin to think about a question that often is overlooked, but frequently is of critical importance, in matching ministers and congregations.

Second, he opened the door for the fourth part of the answer to his earlier question when he asked for suggestions of what he might talk about in his conversation with the people representing St. John's Church.

This has to do with expectations. What do the people at St. John's expect of their next pastor? Of themselves? What can the next pastor expect of St. John's?

Most important of all, what do the people at St. John's understand that God expects of them as a called-out community of believers in today's world?

As Pastor Johnson and the people from St. John's talked, about what should be expected of the minister in a parish such as St. John's, it soon became apparent that each person held different expectations about the role of the next pastor and about the priorities on his gifts, skills, and time.

Thus before they finished discussing expectations they were already into the fifth part of the response to Don Johnson's earlier question about what a pastor should have on his agenda when contemplating a change in pastorates. It deals with pastoral priorities. While this subject belongs in this chapter, the process suggested for looking at this issue can be utilized in many other situations where a pastor and the people are struggling with the question of priorities. Therefore, this subject merits a separate chapter.

3

Pastoral Priorities

"When it appeared that we might want to continue these discussions beyond the exploratory stage," commented the Reverend Mr. Donald Johnson to the seven-member committee representing St. John's Church, "I knew that sooner or later we would be getting into a discussion of the priorities on the time and energies of the person who becomes the next pastor at St. John's. So I sent off for a set of cards that are supposed to facilitate this process.

"Should we take a half hour and work our way through the process that is suggested here?"

"I don't see how it can do any harm," replied the chairman of the committee from St. John's, "and perhaps we'll even learn something."

"Here's a sheet of directions for everyone," continued Pastor Johnson, handing out the instruction sheets, "and here's a set of cards. Now let's walk through the instructions together before we go any further."

When they reached item 4 on the instruction sheet, they agreed that everyone would sort his cards on the basis of "What will have to be the priorities on the time of the

45

VISITING	COMMUNITY LEADER
Calling in the homes of members or at their place of work in a systematic program to meet each member on his/her own turf.	Serving as a volunteer leader in the community to help make this a better world for all God's children.
TEACHING	**THE LEADER**
Teaching the confirmation class, planning and/or teaching classes for church school teachers, teaching in special short-term classes, etc.	Serving as *the* leader in the congregation—the person to whom members turn for advice and guidance on all aspects of the life and work of the congregation.
COUNSELING	**PERSONAL AND SPIRITUAL GROWTH**
Counseling with individuals on personal and spiritual problems, with couples planning to be married, with those who are hospitalized, with other people on personal and vocational problems, etc.	Developing and following a discipline of Bible and other devotional study, participating in programs of continuing education, and helping to plan and lead opportunities for personal and spiritual growth for others.
ADMINISTRATION	**DENOMINATIONAL AND ECUMENICAL RESPONSIBILITIES**
Serving as "executive secretary" of the congregation, working with committees, helping to plan the financial program of the church, working with committees on planning and implementing program, etc.	Carrying a fair share of denominational responsibilities, participating in ecumenical groups and other cooperative bodies. Also enlisting denominational and ecumenical resources for use in the local situation.
EVANGELISM	**LEADING WORSHIP AND PREACHING**
Calling on the unchurched people in the community, bearing witness to the Good News, calling on prospective new members, and training laymen to be evangelists.	Planning and conducting worship services, including sermon preparation and working with others who will participate in leading corporate worship.
A LEADER AMONG LEADERS	**ENABLER**
Serving with the lay leadership as one of the core of leaders in the congregation—each with his/her own unique gifts and each with his/her own special responsibilities.	Helping others identify their own special call to service and ministry and enabling them to respond to that call.

What Are the Priorities?

What are the priorities on the minister's time in your congregation? What does the minister see as the order of priority on his time? What do the members believe it to be? One way to find the answers to these and related questions in your parish is to use a set of cards similar to those shown here. Here is a suggested procedure for using this process.

1. Reproduce enough copies so each member of the committee will have one sheet listing the priorities on the pastor's time in your parish.

2. Call together six to eight leaders in your congregation—the people who served on the pulpit committee when the present pastor was called, or on the pastor/parish relations committee or its equivalent.

3. Cut the sheet so each person has one set of cards; distribute these packs of cards to the people around a table.

4. Clarify the ground rules. Is the question "What *are* the priorities on the pastor's time in this congregation?" or "What *should* be the priorities?" or something else? Make sure everyone is responding to the same question.

5. Give everyone from five to ten minutes to look at the cards and sort them out, discarding what he believes to be the four *lowest* priorities on the pastor's time or the least important functions. *Without discussing what they are doing or the reasons for their choices,* each person should arrange the remaining cards in the order of importance.

6. Begin with one of the laymen and moving in rotation around the table ask each person to lay down his top priority card, face up on the table. While doing this, let each person state what he has chosen as the top priority and why. Continue around the table until everyone has placed his top priority card on the table. (It is often helpful if the minister is the last to show his card.)

7. Discuss what the cards reveal. Are they all the same? Are there differences? If so, what do the differences suggest?

8. Continue the same pattern, with each person laying his second priority card just below the one placed on the table earlier. Discuss what the trend appears to be.

9. Continue with six more rounds.

10. Look at the four cards each person discarded earlier. Is there anything resembling a consensus in the discards?

Use this in any way you wish as a tool to stimulate creative and constructive discussion. Have fun!

new pastor at St. John's for the next year or two?" Each person agreed that this was not a discussion of what the priorities would be under ideal conditions, but what the priorities should be in light of the existing situation.

It happened that as they gathered around a table the chairman was sitting to Pastor Johnson's left, so it was agreed that the rotation for each round would begin with the person sitting on Don's right. Thus the chairman would be the seventh person in the rotation and Don would be the last one to turn over his cards in each round.

After everyone had had ample time to study the twelve cards in his deck and arrange them in order, face down on the table with the top priority card on the top of the deck, the man on Don's right was invited to turn over his top priority card and simply call out the name of the function or task.

"Visiting," said this first man.

"Teaching," called out the second member of the committee as she turned over her card.

"Enabler," announced the third.

"Leading worship and preaching," said the fourth.

"The leader," called out the fifth person in a very positive tone of voice.

"Leading worship and preaching," was the sixth person's first priority.

"Leading worship and preaching," said the chairman.

"Leading worship and preaching," said Don as he turned over his top card.

"Well, I see four of us are Christians," declared the sixth man in the rotation. "Leading worship and preaching is the basic reason a minister is set apart by ordination and that should be the first priority on his time."

"I was reared in the Presbyterian Church," spoke up the lady who was second in the sequence, "and there the minister is ordained as a teaching elder while the ruling elders are ordained from among the ranks of the laity in the congregation. I have always believed this was both symbolically and biblically the right way to do it. I think the first priority on a minister's time should be his teaching responsibilities."

"Now let's remember the ground rules," commented the man to Don's right. "We agreed that we would arrange these cards in the light of existing circumstances at St. John's, not in terms of how the world ought to be. Let's face it. The first priority on the new pastor's time at St. John's is to be a pastor to every member, and this means he has to do a lot of calling. At least a dozen families have said to me they feel St. John's has been without a pastor for at least five years."

"There's a lot of truth in what you say," agreed the fifth man in the rotation, "but I came out with a slightly different diagnosis. I think what St. John's needs is a pastor who is a real leader, a 'take charge' type of person. If we don't find that kind of minister the downward curve at St. John's is going to get steeper!"

"Now you're raising a very basic issue," announced the third person to Don's right, "and that's the question of leadership style. What you're suggesting is a top priority on what is clearly becoming an obsolete style of ministerial leadership. We're not looking for a minister who will be *the* leader in St. John's. What we need is a person who sees the role of the pastor as *one* of the leaders in the congregation. This means the top priority on the new pastor's time and talent is as an enabler. That's the style of leadership we need at St. John's today and tomorrow!"

"Perhaps it will help if we move on to the second card," suggested the chairman. "That should tell us whether we're as divided as we appear to be right now."

"Counseling," called the first man to Pastor Johnson's right, as he turned over his second card.

"Leading worship and preaching," said the lady who had placed teaching as the top priority.

"A leader among leaders," announced the man who had advocated enabler as the top priority.

"Evangelism," said the fourth man.

"Administration," called out the man who had given top priority to the role of the pastor as *the* leader.

"Visiting," announced the sixth man, adding, as he nodded in the direction of the man to Don's right, "I'm with Jack over here, what St. John's needs is a pastor who can relate to the people on their own agenda. Our last minister was always so busy with his own agenda he never had time for anyone else's concerns. I put leading worship and preaching first, but among the choices we have here, visiting and counseling are going to be close seconds this first year or two."

"Administration," declared the chairman in a firm tone of voice as he turned over his second card. "A month ago I would have put teaching in second place, but after thinking about the questions Pastor Johnson has been asking us, I'm convinced that administration is second to leading worship and preaching. I'll bet that's what your second card says, too," he added as he turned to Pastor Johnson.

"No, I'm afraid not," replied Don as he turned over his next card and called out, "Enabler."

"Hey, I knew all along you're the man we're looking for," exclaimed the third man to Don's right, who had been arguing in favor of an enabler style of ministerial leadership as the wave of the future.

As the group continued with the next six rounds a three-way split among the committee members from St. John's became increasingly apparent. Two were clearly placing the top priority on a pastoral role that would give the greatest emphasis to healing the wounds at St. John's. Three were united around a high priority for the traditional functions of worship leader, teacher, and evangelist, while two made it clear that the most urgent need was for strong, aggressive leadership and administrative skills.

When the group later examined the stack of discards they found two additional interesting patterns. First, the discards contained eight "Denominational and Ecumenical Responsibilities" cards, seven "Community Leader" cards, six "Visiting" cards, and three "Evangelism" cards. In other words there was a comparatively high degree of agreement that the first three of these functions of the ministry were very low on the priority list at St. John's. In this respect this was a representative group, since both laymen and pastors usually give a very low ranking to "Community Leader" and "Denominational and Ecumenical Responsibilities."

The other pattern revealed by this examination of the discards was that "The Leader" card had been discarded by four persons, one of whom was Pastor Johnson. The other four laymen from St. John's had discarded "A Leader Among Leaders." This again is consistent with a general pattern which usually finds a majority of ministers supportive of the "Enabler" and "A Leader Among Leaders" emphasis on leadership, while a majority of laymen tend to prefer a minister who is willing and able to be *the* leader in the parish.

There are at least four useful values in this process of determining the priorities people place on the various roles and responsibilities of a pastor.

The most obvious is that it gives everyone an equal vote. No one person can dominate the process of setting priorities. In a discussion format the individual who speaks most eloquently or has a very forceful personality often can sway some members of a group. In this process each has to do his own ordering of the priorities and then live with his decision. Once a person lays his stack of cards face down on the table he gains a degree of invulnerability to being influenced by the priorities of others.

Closely related to this is the usefulness of this process in opening up differences in value systems that might otherwise be concealed by the rhetoric of a few and the silence of others. Once these differences are literally out on the table for all to see they are easier to deal with.

A third value is that the process tends to lift up with high visibility the very low priorities in the value systems of a majority, which never get attention because so often all the time is devoted to a debate over the top priorities.

Finally, this process tends to challenge the common assumption that "we're all in agreement on what we're looking for in a new pastor; now our real job is to find the minister who can meet our specifications."

This came through very clearly here in the work of the committee from St. John's Church. After they had finished examining all the cards, the chairman turned to Don and said, "Pastor Johnson, frankly I don't know whether you're the minister for us, or whether St. John's is the right parish for you. I do know, however, that you have done us two major favors tonight. The first was when you asked all those 'why' questions as you reviewed the statistical record from St. John's.

"The second was when you used these cards to help me see an important fact. I am not really the chairman of one committee, but the chief honcho of three small subcommittees—each with its own set of priorities—that have been masquerading as one committee. We really do not have a right to sit down and talk seriously with any minister about coming to St. John's until we do a better job on our own homework and come to some agreement on what kind of minister we're really looking for. We're in your debt, sir, for helping us to see that we still have a lot of work to do."

With these comments the chairman highlighted a point that frequently is overlooked when a minister meets with a pulpit committee. Unless he is so eager to leave where he is that he cannot be burdened with this additional responsibility, the pastor being interviewed by a pulpit committee should try to help that committee as it carries out its responsibilities. It is reasonable to expect the minister being interviewed to help the pulpit committee improve its skills, its understanding of the task that has been assigned to it, and its capabilities to carry out that assignment in a responsible and effective manner.

The pastor, if he does move to the new parish, probably will have many occasions in the years ahead to be grateful that he did help uncover inconsistent expectations, and did bring up sensitive subjects when he was still seen as an "outsider." He will never have that same type of freedom once he becomes the pastor at that church.

Even if he does not move to the new parish, the time and effort spent in working with the committee to help them identify issues and to raise important questions may yield valuable benefits for his brother in the ministry who does become the next pastor of that parish.

Postscript

The process for discussing and defining priorities that has been presented in this chapter was developed for use by pulpit committees and prospective pastors as they met to discuss mutual expectations. It has been used widely for that purpose. The procedures and the categories suggested here represent the fourth revision in the development of the process.

Any layman or minister who would like to use this process is free to copy it as presented here. He also is free to adapt it by rephrasing or replacing some or all the categories to fit more precisely the local circumstances. To be more directive, the reader is not only free to make such adjustments as are appropriate to the local circumstances, but is strongly urged to make them!

Another point at which this process can be helpful is at the time of the "review" meeting between the new pastor and several leaders from the congregation, usually scheduled approximately six months to a year after the new pastor arrives on the scene.

Pastor Johnson eventually did agree to go to St. John's. A week before he moved he wrote the chairman of the committee and asked that such a review meeting be scheduled for a specific time and place approximately six months later. In his letter he also listed six items that he wanted to be sure would be on the agenda for that meeting, and he urged the chairman to have his committee to do likewise so that at least a major portion of what would be discussed would be defined early. Pastor Johnson felt that setting the date and formulating at least part of the agenda would reduce the chances for speculative comments such as these: "I hear the new pastor met with the pulpit committee last night. You don't suppose he is resigning already, do you?" "Now why in the world does he want to bring that up at this time?" "I wonder what she really means when she asks that question."

Among the six items Pastor Johnson wanted on the agenda were a discussion of his role as a community leader, an evaluation of his preaching, an evaluation of casual "drop-in" visiting, a review of possibilities for in-service training opportunities for laymen, and a period of time for talking through the process on determining pastoral priorities, using a set of cards that would be especially tailored to the situation at St. John's.

It should not be assumed, however, that the process described here is limited to discussions between a pastor and a group of laymen on the priorities on the minister's time and talents.

It can be and has been adapted to many other types of occasions when a group of people have to assign priorities among a range of demands. These include the priorities in the local church budget, the priorities among the goals of the Christian education program, the expectations a United Methodist bishop has for the district superintendents in his cabinet, the priorities in the denominational budget, and the priorities on the time of the staff of a regional judicatory. In each case the basic values described earlier make this a useful procedure.

4

The Interim Pastorate

It was while he was in the preliminary conversations with the representatives from St. John's that Pastor Johnson began to think about the alternatives open to him if he did move.

One of the events that sparked his thinking was the conversation of several of his fellow pastors one night after the evening session at an overnight meeting of a denominational committee. As Don and a dozen other ministers sat in the dining hall drinking coffee about ten o'clock that evening, one of the clergymen asked, "Does anyone else here know what it feels like to be an interim pastor?

"The reason I ask," he continued, "is that I am just discovering that this may be my own situation. A year and a half ago I came to Calvary to follow Dr. Henry Rogers, who had been the pastor there for nineteen years. I've about decided that my role is to serve as the transition between yesterday and tomorrow. For nineteen years that parish was built around the image of one man. Dr. Rogers was a strong leader, and the people simply followed his lead or got out. Anyone here know what I'm talking about?"

"I hear you, friend," spoke up another minister. "Several years ago I followed a man who had been the pastor of that congregation for twenty-eight years. I went there expecting that I, too, might stay twenty-eight years. I left after less than two years. After a few months I realized I had but two choices. I could try to follow in the steps of my predecessor and do things the way they had always been done, or I could break the mold, make a lot of people unhappy by encouraging new people to move into leadership roles, help introduce some new ideas, and then get out. I chose the latter. I left six years ago. A couple of months ago I got a tremendous letter of thanks from the minister who followed me. He wrote that he was just beginning to realize how I had helped make possible the wonderful ministry he is having there. He confirmed what I felt at the time, that that situation needed an interim pastor who would shake things up, open the doors to change, and then move on, carrying the hostility away with him."

"While my situation was different from what you two are talking about, I spent nineteen months as an interim pastor a few years ago," added another minister. "I followed a brilliant young minister who had died at thirty-three after a two-year, losing battle with cancer. His widow stayed in the community and taught school. The problem I had was that this man was 'present' far more than if he had moved to another parish. I dare say that during that first year two-thirds of the conversation in all the calls I made was about what a tragedy this was and how well the widow was adjusting. At least half the homes had his picture on the piano or the television set or the wall. For six months I was about the most frustrated preacher you ever saw. These people had canonized this fellow who had died so prematurely, and I was trying to follow a god, not another mere mortal.

"After about six months," he continued, "I finally woke up to what was happening; so I deliberately spent the next year trying to help these people talk through their grief. I worked with the widow as she sought a place as a director of Christian education in another state, and I did all I could to help that parish get ready for another pastor."

"What do you think should have happened in that situation?" inquired Don.

"This is only the seven-hundredth time I've thought about that question," came the immediate response. "In my opinion, the leadership of the denomination should have encouraged that congregation to bring in an older minister—a retired military chaplain, for example—for six to eight months. He could have helped the people to work through their grief and to serve as a support group for this young widow. After several months he could have led them to begin to think about the future. As it was, I spent nineteen months doing accidentally—and probably rather clumsily—what could have been accomplished more effectively in one-third that time."

"You sound a little bitter," said one of the other men who had been listening in on the discussion.

"I don't think I'm bitter," came the reply, "but I know I'm smarter. We should all be more alert to these situations than we tend to be, and we should be more careful in what happens. For example, right now we have this huge supply of chaplains who have retired after twenty or thirty years in the military. One of those men could have been asked to move into this situation and serve as a combination pastor, father-figure, and counselor for a few months, until the people were ready to move on to the next chapter."

"Maybe that's what should have been done in my last pastorate," said another of the group in a reflective tone. "I hadn't thought about it in these terms until tonight's discussion began, but I served a rather frustrating pastorate for four years before I moved to my present church.

"This may sound unbelievable," he continued, "but my predecessor in that church had come in September to follow a minister who had left his wife and run off with a member of the choir the previous June. Everyone was delighted when my predecessor arrived, because he had a lovely wife and two wonderful children, and was obviously a strong family man.

"By now you can guess what happened," he continued slowly to what was now a very intent audience. "One night, fourteen months after this fellow's arrival, he disappeared with a married woman from the choir."

"What I want to know," interrupted one of the ministers, "is how come your wife agreed that you should go to a church with that kind of choir?"

"By the time I got there things were in bad shape. A lot of people had quit the church, attendance was down to half what it had been three years earlier, the church was the butt of jokes all over town, and some people were talking about closing the doors," continued the former pastor of this demoralized congregation. "I have always been an activist, so I started right in to rebuild the program and to get the people's attention off the past and on the future. I often said to my wife that our job was to replace gossip with the gospel, and backbiting with soul-searching. Along about the third year things began to move, but when the chance came to move from there to where we are now, I was glad to grab it.

"Now after hearing what you fellows have said, I'm beginning to get a new perspective on that situation. Maybe I was a four-year interim pastor in a situation that really needed about six months to a year with a solid, stable, mature minister who would help people talk through their problems and their distrust. Maybe if I had followed a short pastorate like that," he concluded reflectively, "I might have had a much more creative ministry in that situation."

As he listened to this conversation Don began to ask himself if he should ask the people from St. John's whether they were looking for an interim pastor or seeking a minister who would come with the expectation of staying for several years.

While this question actually had little relevance for the situation at St. John's Church, it is a very relevant question. Whenever a change in pastors is under immediate consideration, all three parties to the new arrangement should ask themselves the question, "Is this a situation in which it might be wise to consider an interim pastorate of from six to twenty-four months to serve as a bridge between what was and what is to come?"

The leaders in the parish should ask themselves this question. The appropriate denominational executive should *always* ask this question of himself, and occasionally of leaders in the parish, when this appears to be a possibility. The prospective pastor, especially if he is eager to leave where he is, should ask it before agreeing to move.

If he does not, his next move may be out of the pastorate. Some of the most serious cases of professional disillusionment and personal frustration have resulted from a pastor's moving into what he believed to be a permanent pastorate when the real need was for an interim pastor.

There are at least six types of parish situations in which the concept of an interim pastorate merits serious consideration.

The most common is that in which the pastor who has served his congregation for over fifteen years dies or retires. In approximately four out of five such parishes, regardless of whether the pastor dies or retires after his fifteen or twenty or thirty or forty years there, the next minister is an interim pastor. Not infrequently the new pastor does not recognize this, and he stays too long, does too little, and then leaves, a puzzled, wounded, and frustrated person. In perhaps one out of five of these long, terminal pastorates the way has been paved for the next pastor to come in and have a creative, fruitful, and rewarding pastorate.

The second type of parish where an interim pastorate may be appropriate is closely related to the first. It is the church whose pastor, after fifteen or twenty years' service, moves on to another parish or to some nonparish position. His successor faces more favorable odds than the first type, but, in a majority of the cases studied, the next minister also is an interim pastor—though frequently he does not realize it until several years later.

A third type frequently overlaps the first two, and can be seen most clearly in terms of leadership styles. The Christian churches in the United States, both Catholic and Protestant, have encouraged a strong authoritarian style of leadership. This style of leadership is suddenly experiencing a sharp decline in popularity.[1] The growing demand is for a collaborative style of leadership in which the pastor is seen as *one* of the leaders in the parish, rather than *the* leader. The demands for German language services and for the *Herr Pastor* type of ministerial leadership are both on the decline, but in both cases nostalgia keeps them from disappearing completely.

In this trend of change in style of leadership some parishes have found an interim pastorate the quickest and easiest means of shifting from the strong authoritarian style that has been the pattern for decades to a more open and collaborative style of leadership with a broader base of participation and a greater emphasis on recognizing the gifts and talents of laymen. One of the most common illustrations of this is the large parish whose very authoritarian pastor dies or retires after fifteen or twenty years of service and is followed by a minister who sees himself as one member of a team ministry and as one of the leaders of the parish. Unless adequate attention is given to the tensions and frustrations that are a part of this transition in leadership style, the new minister may find himself to be an interim pastor, often much to his surprise. Incidentally, such situations usually can be identified very easily by the procedure described in chapter 10. When this procedure reveals that the leaders ascribe 50 or 60 or 70 percent of the influence in the decision-making process to the senior minister, it may be time to consider an interim pastor for the transition period that will follow his departure.

[1] For an elaboration on changes in leadership see Lyle E. Schaller, *The Change Agent* (Nashville: Abingdon Press, 1972), pp. 123-31. See also Gerald J. Jud, "The Local Church and the Big Daddy Fantasy," *Crisis in the Church*, ed. Everett C. Parker (Philadelphia: Pilgrim Press, 1968), pp. 39-49.

A fourth type of situation in which an interim pastor may be appropriate was described earlier by the minister who had followed the thirty-three-year-old pastor who died of cancer.

Another type can be placed under the general label of "major internal disturbances." One example of this was described by the pastor who had followed two ministers who had found the church choir an attractive recreational scene. Another is the parish that experiences a financial disaster. A third is the parish where the minister was charged with heresy and the trial dragged on for two years.

A sixth type of situation where an interim pastorate may be the appropriate bridge between two eras is the parish that has been functioning in much the same way for decades, but now, it is clear to an increasing number of people, needs major changes. An example is the white congregation in a community into which an increasing number of blacks or Spanish-speaking persons are moving. Another is the parish that persists in perpetuating yesterday's patterns in the face of growing indifference, because "we have a good thing going—it's been working for years and we aren't going to take any risks by changing it." A third example of this type of situation is the small and long-established rural parish which finds itself surrounded by newcomers moving out from the city. Another example is old First Church downtown, which is faced with the choices of dying, relocating, or developing a new role for itself.

In each of these examples an intentional interim pastorate of six months to two years may help bridge the transitional period.

While there are many persuasive arguments that can be

offered against this concept of an interim pastorate, many of them overlook one of the central tenets of good parish administration. There are occasions when the "one thing at a time" agenda should be followed very carefully. Frequently the person who has the greatest freedom to ensure that first things are done first and the agenda is not overloaded is the minister who knows before he arrives on the scene that he is to be an interim pastor.

Perhaps the most frequently asked question about this concept is "How can we prevent our new minister's tenure turning unnecessarily into an interim pastorate?" The best response to that question is to suggest that both clergymen and parish leaders recognize that some situations call for an interim pastor and that others will turn into that type of situation if too much is expected of the new minister in his first several months in the parish.

5

The Pastor's Compensation

Recently two Presbyterian ministers returned home after a short trip out of town. As the first one walked into his home he received an enthusiastic welcome from his wife, who reported joyfully, "There's a letter for you from St. Andrew's Church." On opening the envelope the minister found an invitation from the chairman of the pulpit committee of that congregation asking him to come for a second interview to discuss the terms of a possible call.

With both hope and fear in her voice his wife urged, "You're going to go, aren't you? If they extend a call, we can move out of this dump and get into a decent manse that has enough room for our family."

Two hours after the second minister arrived home his wife casually mentioned to him, "Oh, I guess I forgot to lay it out, but there's a letter for you from Westminster Church. I wouldn't be surprised if they're asking you to come back and meet with their pulpit committee again. I don't know why they're so persistent. They saw this house, and I can't understand why they would expect us to want to move out of this new home into that hundred-year-old shack they call a manse at Westminster!"

These two illustrations lift up one of the most neglected factors, which also is often an extremely crucial element in the "compensation package" received by the effective pastor—a happy wife.

The congregation can contribute to the pastor's wife's happiness in many ways, including such variables as viewing her as another member of the congregation rather than a supply of free clerical labor and allowing her the same freedom to say no that is granted other members. Another contribution to the personal well-being of the minister's wife is providing a good residence for the minister and his family. The minister's spouse who is happy in her role as the wife of a clergyman can be a major asset to his ministry. The wife who is unhappy with her role or discontented with the housing can be an inhibiting factor in her husband's ministry.

As the representatives from St. John's Church talked among themselves, they decided they would offer Pastor Johnson and his wife their choice of a housing allowance or the use of the church-owned parsonage.

"Let's give them a choice and let them make the decision," advocated Jack Peterson. "In the meantime we can concentrate on such questions as salary, car allowance, and other items."

"I had a chance to talk about pastors' salaries with Paul Peters from the denominational office the other day," added Everett Wright, "and I think we should work up a list of items so we don't forget anything. I'm convinced that Pastor Johnson is the man we're looking for, and I don't want any neglected little detail breaking up what looks to me to be a promising relationship. I believe in getting every question settled in advance so there won't be any misunderstandings later on."

"I'll second that," said Betty White. "Let's start making out our list."

After meeting among themselves for two evenings, the committee from St. John's agreed on the following list, as they prepared for what they hoped would be their final meeting to complete the arrangements with Pastor Johnson.

1. Cash salary —An annual rate of $9,000 per year for the balance of this calendar year and a $700 increase effective the first of next year.

2. Car allowance —$150 per month, based on the assumption that the pastor at St. John's would have to travel 15,000 miles a year on church business.

3. Insurance —The parish to pay both the parish's and the pastor's share of the denominational health, accident, and liability insurance program for ministers.

4. Pension —The parish to pay the whole 13 percent of the pastor's salary required by the denominational pension program.

5. Book and periodical allowance —The parish to pay up to $150 per year for subscriptions to professional and religious periodicals and for books.

6. Continuing education—In accordance with the denominational plan, the parish to "deposit" two weeks' time and $100 in cash each year in a continuing education "bank." Pastor Johnson could "spend" this each year or allow it to accumulate; for example, at the end of four years he could "withdraw" eight weeks of educational leave time and $400. The denomination was prepared to match the parish dollar for dollar up to $100 per year, and the minister, as a professional, was expected, to pay part of the total cost.

7. Vacation —Two weeks for the balance of this year,

three weeks next year, and four weeks each year beginning with the second full year.

8. Housing —A choice of $3,000 per year in a housing allowance *or* use of the church-owned parsonage with the parish paying for all utilities and maintenance.

9. Moving expenses —St. John's to pay the cost of moving expenses up to a maximum of $800.

10. Sick leave —The pastor to be granted one day of sick leave each month, and he can accumulate this up to a total of 120 days. In order to discourage casual use of sick leave the parish will make a payment of one month's salary for each two months of unused sick leave when the pastoral relationship is terminated.

As they looked over the list, near the end of the second evening, Jack Peterson commented, "I feel kind of like a fool walking into a meeting with a minister and laying a list such as this on the table. I'm especially embarrassed by the items on vacation, moving expenses, and sick leave. This list makes it look like we think we're some big corporation, and not just a friendly little church. I still think we ought to say simply that we'll pay his moving expenses, whatever they turn out to be, give him three or four weeks' vacation every year, and, if he gets sick, we'll take care of him. We're looking for a pastor, not an executive."

"I'm willing to discuss any changes you want to suggest," replied Everett Wright, who had been the leader in drafting the list, "but I'm firmly convinced that the fairest way to begin an arrangement with a new pastor is to do everything we possibly can to prevent any future misunderstandings. After fifteen years as a personnel officer I'm convinced the best way to do that is to try to foresee as many contingencies as possible and at least to arrive at a tentative agreement."

"I kind of agree with Jack," interjected Betty White, "but I believe everything on our list belongs there. It does look terribly impersonal, though. Maybe what we should do is call Pastor Johnson, tell him we're coming to next week's meeting with a list of items to be discussed, and urge him to bring his own list. Maybe that way we'll not look so businesslike, and we'll also get some ideas from him."

The committee agreed to follow Mrs. White's suggestion, and the chairman telephoned Don and asked him to come prepared with his list.

To say the committee was a little startled when they compared Pastor Johnson's list with their own is something of an understatement! To begin with, they had felt somewhat guilty about bringing in a list with ten items on it. Pastor Johnson's list had twice as many:

1. An agreement that this committee or an appropriate successor group to be named by the church council will meet with the pastor for two hours six months after his arrival at St. John's, to discuss (a) the congregation's expectations of him and his performance and (b) his expectations of St. John's.

2. An agreement that such a review committee will meet with him every six months thereafter.

3. St. John's will provide thirty hours of paid secretarial service each week.

4. The pastor will be encouraged to spend four days a year visiting other congregations to see what they are doing and to learn what he can that will help him in his ministry at St. John's.

5. At least two laymen will accompany him on two days of these visits every year.

6. The church council will agree to an overnight, Friday-

evening-and-all-day-Saturday planning retreat at least once a year.

7. At least one-half of the church council will participate in some kind of in-service training program for laymen every year.

8. The parish will include at least $600 in the budget each year to pay for lay training events.

9. The pastor's wife will be expected to be a member of St. John's parish, no more, no less.

10. For every call the pastor makes on members *or* non-members, laymen from the congregation will make at least one call.

11. There will be an annual accounting of these calls to the parish by *both* the pastor and the lay callers.

12. The parish will participate in the denominational program for the continuing education of pastors. (This was the same as the committee's item 6.)

13. The parish will pay all utilities at the parsonage.

14. The beginning cash salary will be $9,000 per year.

15. St. John's will pay ten cents a mile for church-related travel.

16. St. John's will pay the monthly cost of the denominational pension program.

17. St. John's will pay the full premiums in the denominational health insurance program.

18. St. John's will pay all expenses of this move.

19. Vacation time will be three weeks per year, *in addition* to time for continuing education events and for Don's obligations as a counselor at summer church camp.

20. St. John's will agree to pay the parish's share of the cost for Don to spend four days in the denominational career counseling center after he has had five years of service at St. John's.

As she compared these two lists Betty White exclaimed, "I was afraid I would be embarrassed by our being too businesslike and precise in our list, but your list really is far more comprehensive and specific than ours. I guess I'm embarrassed at how much emphasis we placed on economic considerations, while your list is dominated by concerns about ministry and what you expect of us."

"Please don't feel embarrassed," replied Pastor Johnson. "When you asked me to make up a list I started to think in terms of salary, pension, insurance, and vacation. Then it occurred to me that here was a unique opportunity to talk about what I'm really concerned about in terms of compensation. My list really breaks down into three parts. The first deals with what I call satisfactions. Several items, such as 1, 2, 11, and 20, fit into that category. I want to know how I am doing in my job and to have the satisfaction not only of doing the job, but also of getting some honest evaluations of my work. Overlapping that first category are my concerns for strengthening the lay ministry of the church. I've mentioned these before. I decided we would understand each other better if you could see what my expectations are of the people at St. John's.

"Finally," continued Pastor Johnson, "I thought I should include what I expected you would want me to put on my list when we talk about compensation."

As they discussed the two dozen items on the two lists, the members from St. John's and Pastor Johnson agreed that he was the minister they were seeking and that this was the place for his next pastorate, as well as agreeing on his compensation. Perhaps more important, however, was the fact that they also came to a better understanding of each other's expectations than they might have achieved had they come together simply to discuss salary.

6

Parsonage
or Housing Allowance?

"Now that the salary question is settled, there is one more question we need to discuss before we're ready to come to a final agreement," the chairman of the committee from St. John's Church said to the Reverend Donald Johnson after he had agreed to become the next pastor of the suburban St. John's congregation. "Which would you prefer, to live in the parsonage three doors down the street from the church, or to receive a housing allowance? We have a firm offer from a family that would like to purchase the parsonage at a fair price, but we're under no pressure to sell. It's up to you. We'll supply a four-bedroom parsonage and pay all utilities, or we'll pay you $3,000 a year as a housing allowance and you can be a taxpayer like the rest of us. What's your preference?"

A week earlier Don had been talking with a seminary classmate who told him he had purchased a house for $22,000 in 1965 with a $4,000 down payment and had just sold it for $32,000—a $10,000 profit on a $4,000 investment. "You can't do that well in the stock market," was his closing remark to Don as they parted company.

"Could I call you Friday after my wife and I have had time to talk this over?" was Don's response to the question.

The possibility of receiving a housing allowance instead of living in a church-owned parsonage was not a new idea for Don Johnson. He and his wife had talked about it on several occasions. Both were aware of a general trend among ministers in which an increasing number were choosing to receive a housing allowance rather than occupy a manse or parsonage owned by the parish. In some cases, the congregation proposed this arrangement, typically when the parsonage next door to the church either was razed or was remodeled for use as a parish hall, or when the congregation decided to upgrade the quality of the pastor's housing. More often the change was initiated by the pastor.

This trend toward paying a housing allowance instead of providing a parsonage appears to be growing most rapidly in new congregations, in theological seminaries and specialized ministries, among pastors in the United Presbyterian Church USA and the United Church of Christ, and among denominational staff members. It appears to be growing at a somewhat slower pace among pastors in such denominations as The United Methodist Church, The Christian Church, and several Lutheran bodies.

Why would a pastor prefer a housing allowance to "free" housing?

There are many answers to that question, but before looking at these it may be helpful to note two considerations that often are overlooked in this discussion.

First, the church-owned parsonage or manse is an arrangement that exists *primarily as a convenience to the congregation,* not to the pastor. This is why the minister does not have to pay federal income tax on the value of his housing. Traditionally, the arrangement has been the result of the congregation's desire to have a resident minister.

Second, a sense of "belonging" to a familiar place is very important to human beings. Only recently has this truth begun to receive the consideration it deserves. Many pastors, ministers' wives, and "preachers' kids" express concern that they have been denied this opportunity to feel a sense of place.

In reviewing the most frequently mentioned reasons that a minister prefers to receive an adequate housing allowance instead of a "free" house, one consideration usually stands out above all others—his desire for the opportunity to build an equity in a house so he will be able to buy his own home when he retires. Closely related to that is the desire to take advantage of the inflationary trend of this era.

Other reasons include a desire for privacy, the opportunity to be seen and to function as a tax-paying homeowner in the community, to pick a house that meets the family's needs and tastes, and to be free from dependency on a parsonage committee that may not function as effectively as desired.

These are impressive and persuasive reasons. Why would any pastor not choose this alternative? Why would he prefer to live in a church-owned house rather than his own home?

Two reasons are illustrated by the experience of another friend of Don's who began receiving a housing allowance from the congregation he had been serving for several years. He bought a home for $23,500 in September with a 10 percent down payment. He unexpectedly moved to another congregation the following March. His family continued to live in the house, partly to enable the children to complete the school year and partly because a house without furniture is harder to sell than one which is occupied. Finally, in the following November, he was able to sell the house for $22,000. After paying the realtor's commission and related selling costs, his equity was slightly under $100. In addition to being separated from his family for eight months, he had seen his personal savings decreased by over 95 percent. This pastor would not go to a church that expected the minister to buy his own home!

This incident illustrates two of the three major reasons some pastors prefer not to receive a housing allowance. First, it either reduces their mobility or it may make it more difficult to move. Second, while it is possible to make money in a rising market, it also is possible to lose money in a declining market. For example, in several metropolitan areas with unusually high unemployment it is very difficult to find a buyer for a house who will pay anywhere near the market price of that home two or three years ago. It also is very easy to lose money on an investment in a home in any of two dozen large, central cities in the northeastern and north central states.

A third reason offered by many pastors is that the housing allowance paid by the church often is far less than the cost of owning a home. For example, one church had been supplying the pastor with a home valued at $25,000 and had paid all utilities (which averaged $700 a year). In that state a church-owned parsonage is exempt from property taxation. This congregation began paying the minister a $3,000-a-year housing allowance. He bought a $30,000 home with a $3,000 down payment and found himself paying $2,200 a year in interest, $750 in general property taxes, $800 a year for utilities, and $80 for insurance. This was in addition to his payments on the principal of the mortgage, which averaged slightly over $700 a year, and his other maintenance costs; and he no longer was collecting $160 a year in interest on his savings, which had gone into the down payment and closing costs. The $3,000 housing allowance began to look less and less attractive, and he wondered how some of his colleagues, who were receiving housing allowances in the $1,500 to $2,400 range, could afford this arrangement.

In addition to these three major reasons, a number of pastors have objected to a housing allowance on other grounds. Many do not have the necessary down payment for a house. Some would prefer to invest their savings in something other than real estate. Several object to the distractions of maintaining a house. A few admit they could never buy a home as expensive as the church-owned parsonage in which they live; thus they can have luxury housing without any disturbance of either their pocketbook or their conscience.

From the congregation's perspective, the issue is equally complex. The congregation that sold its parsonage and pays a housing allowance may find that when the present pastor moves they will feel morally obligated to buy his home and/or find potential candidates are not interested because they either cannot or will not buy their own home. In a few cases, the congregation had loaned the pastor the money to buy his home, and then loaned his successor the money to buy the house from the minister who was leaving. Some members in these congregations are not sure they really are "out of the real estate business."

The congregation in the small community where the inventory of homes for sale or for rent is very limited may find itself in a very difficult situation when the present pastor with a small home moves to another church and puts his house on the market, while the new pastor with a big family requires a larger home than anything that is available in the community.

Many congregations, especially in those states where the parsonage is exempt from the general property tax, have a major problem in paying an adequate housing allowance. First of all, while the leaders may realize that anything less than $3,600 a year is unfair to the pastor, many members will regard anything over $1,800 as exorbitant. Second, and somewhat more subtle, is the plain fact of life that many congregations are more willing to raise money for building than for the operating budget. This means that it may be easier for a congregation to buy a $35,000 manse or parsonage which they feel is "ours" than to raise the necessary money to pay a $2,400-a-year housing allowance so the pastor can buy an $18,000 home.

After several hours of studying and discussing this issue, Don's wife finally exclaimed, "It sure would have been easier if they had simply told us to move into the parsonage and only asked us what color paint they should use in redecorating the living room!"

"They've offered to redecorate if we do decide to move into the parsonage," replied Don, "but that's not the question. By tomorrow noon we have to tell them whether we want a housing allowance or a parsonage."

Finally, they decided to list the arguments for and against moving into St. John's parsonage.

"Should We Move into the Parsonage?"

For

Relieves us of the trouble, cost, and worry of home ownership.

Might be the fairest arrangement for our successor at St. John's.

Perhaps our moving into the parsonage will increase his choices when that day comes.

Improves our vocational mobility.

In this case it is cheaper, since the church-owned house is exempt from the general property tax.

Removes the risk that when we move we will have to sell at a loss.

This parsonage is better than anything we can afford to buy or rent.

The church can more easily raise the money to build (or buy) and maintain a church-owned parsonage than provide a housing allowance.

Since some ministers do not have the down payment necessary to purchase a home, they therefore, could not accept an appointment or call to this church if it did not provide a parsonage.

Against

Buying will enable us to build up an equity in our own home.

Buying will eliminate the need for a parsonage committee.

Buying will give us a choice of the type of housing and location we prefer.

Buying our home will encourage us to stay longer.

We should be seen, and should see ourselves, as home-owning taxpayers.

Buying will allow us to benefit from inflation in housing prices.

Buying will "get the church out of the real estate business."

Buying will enable us to experience one more element of the "real world"—the world of the layman who has to find his housing in the private market.

Buying will enable us to own our home when Don retires.

After agonizing over the pros and cons, Don asked his wife, "Well, what's your preference? We may not have this choice again for a long time."

"It's up to you, Honey," she replied. "I really don't know what to say."

"The personal reasons are heavily on the side of buying our own home," replied Don. "But the professional and financial reasons are in favor of moving into the parsonage. In the first place I think I need to be free to spend as much time as possible being the pastor at St. John's this first year. I don't think I can afford the diversion of buying and maintaining a house. In the second place, every financial expert I've talked to says buying a house is a second-rate method of investing money. With interest rates as high as they are, the men I've talked to consider a house a poor economic investment. In the third place, by moving into the parsonage we maximize the freedom for ourselves, for the congregation, and for our successor when the day comes that we should leave St. John's."

"And in the fourth place," added his wife, "this is the simplest, easiest, and fastest way to settle this issue."

"And in the fifth place," laughed Don, "I believe you really like that parsonage at St. John's."

7

What Do You Pay Your Laymen?

"What do you pay your Sunday school teachers?"

When Pastor Johnson asked this question of the members of the Christian Education Committee at St. John's Church the second week after his arrival, the response was a series of puzzled frowns.

"I suppose there are some congregations that pay their teachers," finally commented Mrs. Boden, "and I suppose it's all right, if that's what they have to do to get enough teachers, but here we've always relied on volunteers. We don't have the money to pay them even if we wanted to, and I don't think we either want to or should pay them."

"When I think of the difficulty we have had in getting volunteers the last few years," added the chairman, "we may have to begin thinking about paying them. Right now we have three teachers who have announced they won't be able to continue in the fall, and there isn't a volunteer replacement in sight."

"If they took their vows as church members seriously," spoke up a grim-faced Mr. Brant, "they should volunteer to work where they're needed in the church and not expect to be paid. That's part of what's wrong with the country today, nobody wants to do anything unless he's paid for it."

This discussion missed the point of Pastor Johnson's original question. *Every church pays its volunteers;* the question is, what does it pay them?

The compensation for volunteer service takes many forms. These include the feeling of satisfaction that often accompanies a positive response to a real need, a sense of personal fulfillment, satisfaction with a job well done, "repayment" for services received from others, reinforcement of a sense of personal worth or value, a response to the obligations incurred by membership in an organization, "brownie points," a channel for expressing neighbor-centered love, prestige, status, public recognition, anticipation of rewards in heaven, "evening the score," fellowship, and the opportunity for personal growth, development, and learning.

A seventy-three-year-old retired farmer, who lives in a town in Nebraska, two or three times a week drives out to the country to help his son with the farm work because "there really is too much for one man to do by himself." This retired farmer's greatest satisfactions come every spring, when he can go out with a huge disk harrow and, in one day, prepare forty or fifty acres for planting. He often contrasts this "good day's work" with what he could accomplish fifty years ago, when he was in his physical prime. In the 1920s in a good day, using a walking plow, he could just begin the preparation of two acres of land for the spring planting. What does his son pay him? Nothing in cash, but a tremendous amount in what the behavioral scientists identify as "psychi rewards."

The importance of psychi rewards or "satisfactions" often is overlooked as the leaders in the local church plan the allocation of volunteer manpower. There are four dimensions to this issue that merit the concern of both the pastor and the people in every congregation. One of these can be illustrated by returning to the conversation at St. John's that was reported in the opening paragraphs of this chapter.

After it was explained that the question included non-financial payments to volunteers, one member added in a very positive tone, "I believe the greatest reward or compensation we could offer a Sunday school teacher would be the guarantee that every Sunday morning he or she will be able to walk into the classroom and find a group of well-behaved and quiet youngsters waiting for the presentation of the lesson."

As soon as the three teachers on the committee recovered from their laughter, one of them responded, "I'm afraid you're dreaming of another planet, Mary. We're not expecting to find a roomful of little angels sitting there when we volunteer as teachers. What we would appreciate, however, would be reasonable working conditions, relevant materials, interesting resources, decent training opportunities, and some counseling help when difficulties arise."

This teacher was lifting up a basic point in her response. The psychi rewards offered volunteers have to be (a) realistic and (b) meaningful or rewarding to the recipient *from the perspective of his own self-perceived needs.*

Another dimension of this issue might be labeled the Golden Rule of Rewarding Volunteers, or "do not return bad for good."

One of the most widespread examples of this is the compensation plan used by many congregations in rewarding persons who volunteer to go out calling. For example, at St. John's Church the practice for several years has been to ask each individual or family to bring to church on Loyalty Sunday the card on which they have recorded their pledge toward the church budget for the coming year. Typically this brings in cards from 70 percent of the households in the parish, some of which are mailed in during the days just before and after Loyalty Sunday.

The finance committee distributed the names of the families from whom no pledge card had been received among fifteen volunteer callers. Each volunteer received five or six cards with instructions for calling at these households and asking for a pledge to the church budget.

While it was not done consciously or deliberately, what had been happening at St. John's was that most of the calls that would have been pleasant, satisfying, and rewarding for these volunteers had been creamed off by the Loyalty Sunday approach. Most of those who would offer an affirmative response when approached had either brought in or mailed their pledge cards. Consequently, four out of five calls made by the volunteers were to persons who were neutral or unhappy in their feelings toward St. John's. If they did sign a pledge card, the decision to do so often was motivated by guilt, by the hard-sell approach of the caller, or by the conclusion that the easiest way to terminate this visit was to sign a pledge card.

There are few satisfactions for the caller in this kind of approach. Had St. John's been more conscious of the compensation it was providing for its volunteer callers, it would have used an every member visitation system. This usually produces a sense of satisfaction and accomplishment for the caller in three or four out of every five calls. Also this plan usually has the fringe benefit of producing from 5 to 15 percent more money in pledges than the approach St. John's has been using.

The same pattern of building in a high level of frustration and dissatisfaction for the volunteers can be found in calling programs directed at members who have not attended worship during the past year, people who are behind schedule in paying the amount they pledged to the church, or people who are not members of the church for the purpose of asking them to contribute time or material toward the annual money-raising event at the church.

A far better method of building a higher level of satisfactions for the caller is to concentrate on calling programs in which the agenda for the call is meeting the needs of the person being called on rather than "pushing our product." This type of calling effort also is far more effective in helping the church identify and respond to the needs of people.

A third aspect of the issue of rewards for volunteers was introduced by the teacher who spoke of her desire for training opportunities.

Pastor Johnson had placed this item on the agenda for the review session scheduled for six months after his arrival at St. John's, but, when the subject came up here, he displayed no hesitation in following up on the opportunity.

"If we think of the feeling of satisfaction that accompanies the completion of a job that has been done well as an important payment for volunteers," he suggested, "perhaps we should place a greater emphasis on the training that enables a person to carry out the task for which they have volunteered."

"That sounds great, but we have tried training programs before, and it's like pulling teeth to get the people who need the training to attend," responded the chairman.

"That's a very widespread problem," agreed Pastor Johnson, "and we'll have to give this some careful consideration, but I am convinced that if we can provide training opportunities in those areas where our leaders and teachers feel they need help, we'll get a response. Too many training programs are developed around what the persons planning the training program *believe* the people need, rather than in response to the real needs of the participants."

Pastor Johnson was correctly identifying one of the critical items in the reward system for volunteers, training opportunities designed to meet the felt needs of the people involved in the training ventures. Churches are notorious for assuming that simply giving a person a title carries with it all the skills necessary to fulfill the responsibilities that accompany the title. This pattern is similar to paying a person with a check that looks very impressive until he takes it to the bank and finds it is worthless.

Later that same evening Pastor Johnson brought up a fourth dimension of this issue when he asked, "What is the procedure for recognizing the contributions of volunteer leadership?"

"Well, we have a commitment service every September for the church school teachers and officers," replied Mrs. Boden. "Is that what you mean?"

"No, I'm thinking of some means of saying thank you to those who have served during the year. What do you do to lift up what had been accomplished and to thank those who helped make these accomplishments possible?"

"Three or four years ago we tried something like what I believe you're suggesting," replied Mr. Brant, "but it didn't work out very well. We had a big banquet here at the church to honor all the volunteers. I was a member of the trustees, and we paid for it out of our own pockets; it didn't cost the church a dime. Eight of us chipped in $400 to pay for this catered meal. It was really a flop, though, and I don't think anyone wants to try that again.

"You see, Reverend," he continued as he addressed the new pastor, "the people here at St. John's really fall into two categories. There's a small group of us who take our church vows seriously and do our jobs because we love the Lord. We don't expect or want or need any special thanks or bouquets. The rest of the people here want to get by as cheaply as they can. They want to do as little as possible—and that includes staying away from a banquet to honor those who do carry the load here."

"I think I hear what you're saying," replied Pastor Johnson, with complete honesty, "and I guess we should postpone any more discussion on this or we won't get through the rest of the agenda."

As he walked down the street from the church to the parsonage later that evening, Pastor Johnson had a strong hunch that he was on the trail of a potential "winner" in this new pastorate.

8

Winners and Losers

"Preacher, I want you to know that, for the first time in my life, world missions has my attention," said the sixty-one-year-old president of the First National Bank, as he wrote out his personal check for $6,500.

As he repeated this comment from one of the parishioners at First Presbyterian, Dr. Frank Harris added, "And that is one part of the story of how we increased our special offering for world missions from $2,700 to $27,000 in one year."

This conversation really had its beginning a few months after Don Johnson came to the pastorate of St. John's Church. He had accumulated since his arrival nearly a dozen items for his "worry list."

This list included a disproportionately low percentage of the total receipts being allocated to the ministry to others; a record of attendance at church council meetings that had averaged between 40 and 60 percent for the past several years; a continuing decline in church school attendance; the experiences with two newcomer families, who joined other churches after they had visited St. John's and found it, in their words, "cold" and "unfriendly"; a real question of whether St. John's should continue the advertisement for the church on the Saturday religion page of the metropolitan newspapers; the leveling off in worship attendance; the clearly apparent decline in the women's organization; the dull youth fellowship; the lack of growth in parish membership in a situation in which all outward signs suggested the parish should be continuing to grow in size and vigor; and the lack of imagination among some of the key leaders.

While he had a few ideas of his own about what needed to be done, Pastor Johnson had decided he would use part of the "honeymoon" while he was new at St. John's to go out and get acquainted with other pastors in the area and see what they were doing that might help him be more effective at St. John's. Therefore, in each conversation with another pastor he injected a question such as "What's happening here that's exciting?" or "What's happened in this parish that has stirred up the people here?" or "What are you doing here that might be of interest to an outsider?"

When he went to see Frank Harris at the First Presbyterian Church he was impressed to learn that this congregation had increased its extra giving to world missions tenfold in one year. He immediately asked, "How?"

"Last year we only raised $2,700 for world missions over and above our regular benevolence budget," replied Dr. Harris. "Some of us thought that was pretty bad for a 2,700-member congregation, only an average of one dollar a member for our special offering for world missions.

"We decided that it was our fault, that our committee had not done enough to dramatize the need, and that we shouldn't blame our people for being cheap. So we decided we would symbolize the whole effort by one part of our special appeal, which was to buy a tractor for one of the new African nations. We borrowed a $6,000 tractor from a dealer here in town and parked it in front of our church one Sunday morning. For some reason or other it didn't get moved for a few days, and one morning a banker came storming in and wanted to know why the custodian was leaving our tractor out in the open, and especially why he had left it in front of the church where it was in people's way when they wanted to get into the building. I suggested that instead of jumping on me he talk to Angus McPherson, who is chairman of our building and grounds committee.

"A day or two later he came back and said, 'Preacher, you knew all along why that tractor was out there. You just set me up when you sent me to see Angus.' I told him I had thought Angus would be able to explain it better than I could," continued Frank Harris.

"Well, to make a long story short, Angus explained to him that as ruling elder he should know that (a) this congregation didn't own a big tractor like that one; (b) the tractor symbolized the special appeal for world missions; and (c) the church was dependent on people like him to make sure this special appeal raised a significant amount of money. So the banker said to me, 'Preacher, what do you think I should be doing about this appeal?' I told him our goal was $25,000 and that one man had offered to contribute fifty cents for every dollar the rest of the congregation contributed. I suggested that if he was serious in asking what he could do he could match the offer of this individual and the two of them together would match the rest of the congregation dollar for dollar. He agreed to do this, and I am firmly convinced that when he wrote out that check for $6,500 he had a greater interest in world missions than he had ever had before."

"Now are you suggesting that this idea of getting a couple of people to match the rest of the congregation on a dollar for a dollar basis is the best way to raise money for world missions?" asked Don Johnson in a somewhat puzzled voice.

"You missed the two key points of my illustration," replied Frank Harris. "What I was trying to emphasize was the importance of a goal and of helping people see where the money is going. A year ago we simply passed out the special offering envelopes and asked people to give whatever they thought appropriate. This year we set a high goal, *and we had the tractor out there so people could see how part of the money would be used.*"

"Furthermore, and I don't think we should overlook this, when our friend wrote out a check for $6,500 for world missions, it motivated him to want to learn a lot more about what the church is doing in world missions. If we had simply permitted him to stick a ten-dollar bill in an envelope some Sunday morning we would have denied him the chance to have his curiosity aroused about what happens to the money. I firmly believe that a man who can write out a check for $6,500 for world missions *should* be curious about what the church is doing and how the money is being used," concluded Dr. Harris.

"What will you do next year?" inquired Don Johnson, in a voice that suggested he was asking how are you going to top this?

"We're working on that now," replied the Presbyterian pastor. "We have four task forces, each composed of six people. One task force will visit Presbyterian work in South America, another, the work in Africa, another, in the Far

90

East, and the fourth will visit some of the mission work here in the United States. Those twenty-four people will compose half of a forty-eight-member committee that will recommend to the session our goal for next year for the special world mission offering. We have $105,000 for benevolences in our regular budget of $340,000. In addition, this year we will have special offerings of at least $90,000 for benevolences over and above the budget. That means that out of total receipts of $430,000 approximately $195,000 will go for benevolences."

"At St. John's they have had a unified budget for years and everything for benevolences is in the regular budget," commented Pastor Johnson. "You're telling me, if I hear you right, that you have both a unified budget *and* special offerings?"

"That's right!" replied Dr. Harris. "Our goal here is to use half our total receipts for benevolences and half for local expenses—and I expect we'll reach that goal in another year or two."

"Couldn't you do it with a unified budget?" asked Don.

"Nope, the unified budget's a loser on that point. The floor becomes a ceiling," replied the Presbyterian pastor firmly. "It may sound like a great administrative idea, but if you're interested in helping the people understand what is happening, how the money is being used, and how they can help as the church responds to the needs of people, the unified budget is a loser and the special offering for designated causes is a winner. Now please don't misunderstand me. I am strongly in favor of building into the regular church budget the denominational asking for benevolences. I'm talking about going beyond simply 'paying our denominational dues.' The unified budget is both a floor and a ceiling on benevolence giving."

91

"But I've always been taught that people don't like to be bothered with special appeals every month or two," objected Don.

"You've been listening to too many preachers," replied Frank Harris. "The *North American Interchurch Study*[1] made it very clear to me that the level of giving is greatly influenced by how clearly the people understand the need. A unified budget tends to conceal needs while a half dozen carefully publicized special offerings each year help people see the needs more clearly. We can't expect every member will give to every special appeal, but when we have six, we are pretty sure we'll offer him one or two opportunities that will coincide with his special concerns. We could never expect to reach a fifty-fifty division between benevolences and local expenses without the advantages of special opportunities for designated giving."

"Let me give you one more example," continued Dr. Harris. "In St. Louis we have a 250-member, biracial congregation in the inner city with receipts from the members of over $50,000 a year. On a per member basis that's nearly twice our national average. When the Central Baptist Church burned down, our Presbyterian congregation had a special offering to help this black, downtown parish rebuild. The session set a goal of $1,000 and decided that if the actual offering was short of this goal, the difference would come out of their current budget. The actual offering was nearly $1,300. That illustrates my basic point again. People do believe in the basic Christian

---

[1] *The North American Interchurch Study* is the report of a study of stewardship based on nearly 3600 intensive interviews conducted in the United States and Canada. Dr. Douglas W. Johnson was the Project Director for this study which was published by the National Council of Churches in November, 1971.

principle of stewardship, but in this day when they are being bombarded with so many requests for money, their natural tendency is to give a token amount unless they see a clearly defined goal to meet a highly visible need."

"Well, thanks for your time," responded Don Johnson gratefully as he stood up to leave. "I think I have several ideas on how to turn a loser into a winner at St. John's."

Later that same morning Don dropped by to see Charlie Williams, who was the pastor of a Presbyterian church in the next municipality. Mr. Williams was arranging a display of color photographs in the church parlor.

"What are you up to today?" inquired Don as he walked in on his perspiring friend.

"Getting ready for the session meeting tonight," came the reply. "Soon after I came here a year ago I suggested that we meet in here instead of in the fellowship hall in the basement. There the session members sat on folding chairs around tables and had a dull, dry, and staid business meeting every month. Half the session members stayed away from it with consistent regularity. When we moved up here where we sat in comfortable chairs in an attractive setting our average attendance for a session meeting jumped from eighteen to thirty-two. That's pretty good considering there are only thirty-six members of the session! So I decided that I should reciprocate by having a different display each month showing what we're doing as a congregation. This month I'm using a bunch of pictures showing what's happening in the Interfaith Housing Park this congregation helped to sponsor."

As he drove home that morning, Don decided he would suggest that St. John's move its monthly meeting of the church council from that barren basement classroom into the church parlor.

A couple of weeks later at the monthly ministerial meeting someone raised the question of the value of newspaper advertisements for a church. A couple of ministers defended them on the basis of their belief that newcomers to the community turned to the Saturday religion page as they began the process of "church shopping." One of them declared that any church that did not have an advertisement in the religion page ran the risk of being left off the lists of these church shoppers.

At this point one pastor challenged the group by asking, "Anyone here know of someone who joined his church because of a church ad in the newspaper?"

After a minute's silence the pastor of Grace United Methodist Church spoke up and said, "While I'm not sure of just why they joined our congregation, I believe that four or five of our recent new members first came to Grace because of our ads in the paper."

"We rarely run an advertisement on the Saturday religion page, however," he added. "As you may have noticed, our ads are scattered. One month we place it in the sports section, another time in the financial pages, another, in the Thursday food section."

"I've always wondered how you got the newspaper to agree to that," inquired another minister. "I've been told that the papers will run church ads only on the Saturday religion page."

"We don't place our ads directly with the newspaper," came the reply from the pastor at Grace. "We place them through an advertising agency headed by one of the members of our congregation. I expect the agency does enough business with the newspapers here that it has some voice in where the ads appear," he added drily. "It was their recommendation that we advertise less often, spend an equal amount of money and run a larger but different ad each month in a different section of the paper. I think it works for us."

"We've dropped our advertising from the newspapers," commented another pastor. "We decided our problem is not one of attracting visitors, but rather of welcoming people who visit our church. For a variety of reasons we get a substantial number of visitors nearly every Sunday. We take the money we save on newspaper advertising and run a six-week training program for our greeters every year. We hire one of these fellows who trains people to develop their memories to remember names and faces."

"You mean greeters, or ushers?" asked Don.

"I mean greeters," responded the pastor who was describing this program. "There is a vast difference between an usher and a greeter. The ushers are invited to come to the training program, but all our greeters are required to attend. The church pays the full cost of this training. A week ago a man came who had visited our church about six months ago. One of our greeters went up to him and said, 'Sure good to see you again, Jack! How's Agnes? I remember David and Laura here, but who's this third youngster? She wasn't with you when you were here before.' That's what I mean about there being a difference between an usher and a greeter. Our greeters know how to greet people, and that man was greeted when he came back to Grace Church."

When he left that meeting of the ministerial association, Pastor Johnson had added two more ideas to the section in his pocket notebook on "winners and losers." He had begun to develop this section of his notebook about two years before he came to St. John's. By Don's definition a "winner" was an idea or procedure or technique that promised creative and productive results, while a "loser" was an approach or procedure that tended to increase the chances of failure, defeat, or frustration.

The first idea that he had proposed at St. John's from his "winners" list was in response to the discussion about compensation for lay volunteers and came out of his own experience back at Trinity Church.

In his third year at Trinity, Pastor Johnson and a group of his lay leaders had agreed that everything was running remarkably smoothly. They agreed that one reason was the large corps of active laymen. Out of their discussion came the plan for a special thanksgiving service the first week in January. This special event consisted of four parts. The first was a special worship service in which the congregation gave thanks to God both for the challenges and opportunities in ministry that had been placed before them during the previous twelve months, and for the resources they had been given to respond to these opportunities. The second part consisted of a series of skits, role-play events, one-act plays, color slides, stunts, vignettes and a fifteen-minute, 8mm movie. These recaptured most of the highlights of the parish for the past year and were arranged to show the range of programs and ministries at Trinity. The third part was a recognition of the contributions of time, energy, talent, money, and skills that had made possible these programs and ministries. The two-hour evening closed with a presentation showing how the things that had been accomplished during the year just ended provided the foundation for the goals and objectives that had been adopted for the coming year.

When Pastor Johnson broached this idea individually to several of the leaders at St. John's, he received a series of very favorable responses. A few weeks later the subject

came up at the monthly church council meeting—the first
to be held upstairs in the church parlor incidentally—and
was adopted with enthusiasm.

After the council meeting, as he walked down the street
to the parsonage, Don was convinced that his first two
suggestions at St. John's had received the reception that
is necessary for an idea to be a winner. Everyone had
agreed that moving the meeting of the church council
upstairs to the more comfortable parlor, where everyone
could sit in a big circle rather than hide behind tables,
should have been done long ago. The creative support
that had emerged for the thanksgiving service next January
suggested that this, too, would be regarded as a winner
the morning after the event itself.

While this was not uppermost in his mind as he walked
from the church to the parsonage, these two suggestions
were, in fact, his second and third winners since arriving
at St. John's. The first, and the one that greatly enhanced
the chances that any suggestions he made at St. John's
would turn out to be winners rather than losers, was the
resolution he had made two years earlier while back at
Trinity to "pay his rent" promptly every week.

Pastor Johnson's reference to "paying the rent"
promptly comes from James Glasse's suggestion that a
congregation wants three things from their minister. They
want him to conduct worship and preach, to be their
pastor and teacher, and to administer the parish. Glasse
contends that (a) paying the rent is not and should not
be seen as a full-time job and (b) if the pastor pays his
rent promptly every week he has considerable discretion
over how he spends the remainder of his time and energy.[2]

[2] Glasse, *Putting It Together in the Parish*, chap. 4.

Don Johnson had spent most of his time and energy in these first months at St. John's in paying the rent promptly, and he was confident this not only gave him control over how he used his discretionary time, but also helped to produce a favorable climate for innovation.[3] While he had personally met his predecessor only briefly on two different occasions, he had learned that St. John's had not been accustomed to a pastor who paid his rent promptly every week.

As he thought further about the future of his ministry at St. John's, he became increasingly convinced that the time had come for him to begin to talk about excellence and quality in the ministry of this parish.

[3] For further reading on the importance of a favorable climate for innovation see Schaller, *Parish Planning*, pp. 65-88, and *The Change Agent*, pp. 54-62.

9

The Quest for Quality

"I read a lot in preparation for this meeting, and I've heard many very interesting and helpful things since we arrived here last night, but the two that stand out in my mind are these sentences from the statement of purpose of a church in Peoria," said Betty White during the first overnight planning retreat to be held in the twenty-five-year history of St. John's Church.

It was Pastor Don Johnson's first September at St. John's Church; twenty-six of the twenty-eight members of the church council had gathered at seven o'clock on Friday evening to begin a twenty-six-hour retreat, in which they focused on the future and the program of their parish. Every person had agreed to read at least one book from a list supplied by Pastor Johnson in preparation for this event. In addition the pastor had gathered statements of purpose from a half dozen congregations and reproduced them so each member of the council had a set.

Mrs. White continued. "The Peoria church's statement says, 'As we translate this mission from understanding to action, we propose to use these objectives for the corporate life of The First United Methodist Church: We shall demand an *excellence of quality* as the first mark of our people and program. We shall recognize the *diversity* of membership and organize our worship and program to meet this variety of needs.' Now there are two concepts we should build into our thinking about the purpose and ministry of St. John's, excellence and diversity."

"I'll buy that," agreed Vernon Watson. "I think an emphasis on excellence and a recognition of diversity should be a part of our style or purpose at St. John's."

"Let's keep the focus on excellence for a few minutes," suggested Bob Smith. "I think we ought to really look at St. John's in the light of that word. I don't think we have actually placed much emphasis on quality. I think our emphasis has been on getting by, not on excellence. Now if we are really serious about this emphasis on quality, we had better think about the costs and the implications."

"I agree with Bob," added Jack Peterson, "there is no question but that quality has a price tag attached to it; however, I don't think we have any choice. All across society there is a new quest for quality. If we ignore this trend, we'll be in trouble."

This discussion among the leaders at St. John's Church lifts up an issue that deserves the serious attention of parish leaders everywhere. The growing interest in the quality of life can be seen, regardless of the direction one looks.[1]

One of the most controversial ventures in public education today is "performance contracting." In this arrange-

---

[1] An excellent introduction to this quest for quality which includes suggestions that can be adapted to the church is Raymond D. Gastil, "Social Indicators and Quality of Life," *Public Administration Review*, November/December 1970, p. 596.

ment a public school board contracts with a private consulting firm to provide specialized instruction in schools where the majority of children are below national educational norms in reading, arithmetic, and other subjects. The consultant is paid only if the educational skills of the pupils increase at an above-average pace. The profit of the consultant is directly dependent upon the students' improved performance.

During the past few years the televised weather forecasts in many metropolitan areas have been altered by the addition of three reports on the quality of the air. These new indices measure the amount of sulphur dioxide, carbon monoxide, dirt, and dust in the air.

The Memphis Chamber of Commerce has developed an entirely new approach in its efforts to attract industry. Formerly, the advertising of the Chamber stressed such traditional factors as location, labor costs, an abundant water supply, and low utility rates. Recent advertisemnts in *Newsweek, Harvard Business Review, Nation's Business, Fortune, The New Yorker, and Town and Country* have included phrases such as "As Memphis has grown bigger, it's grown better"; "We've promoted a quality of life that's creative, enthusiastic, and friendly"; and "Big city style but without big city problems."

Recent magazine advertisements for Japanese Toyota automobiles carry the slogan "We're quality oriented."

These four examples illustrate one of the most important trends of this new decade. This is the quest for quality. From the perspective of the church council members at the planning retreat for St. John's this quest may have a greater impact on the life, program, and ministry of the local church than any other contemporary trend.

In looking at this trend, emphasis should be placed on the word "quest." There is a rapidly growing demand for quality by consumers, but as yet the interest of consumers in quality exceeds the capability of the producers to respond to this growing demand. This disparity is illustrated by the complaints of buyers of new homes or new automobiles. It is illustrated by the growing volume of complaints by parents about the quality of public education, by the difference of opinion between many pastors and laymen on the value of a carefully prepared sermon, and by the conflict between the producers and consumers of environmental pollution.

The growing visibility of the conflict over the importance of quality is another strong indication that the quest for quality is emerging as an important new contemporary trend.

This quest represents a change in the American value system as the emphasis shifts from quantity to quality, from counting activities to measuring performance, and from an emphasis on economy to an emphasis on quality.

The emergence of this quest for quality can be seen in all sections of American society. It can be seen in the demands of blacks and the poor for better schools; the recent rapid growth of the consumer movement; the value system espoused by many young persons; the growing acceptance by the courts of the doctrine of the manufacturer's liability for poorly designed products; the current crusade to protest the pollution of the environment; the rejection by young blue-collar workers of the deadening life on the automobile assembly line; the tremendous acclaim that greeted Charles A. Reich's *Greening of America*, the continued population exodus from the decaying core of the large central cities, the campaign talk of the 1972 presidential election, and the challenges being directed at the traditional goals and practices in institutions of higher education. One example of this new emphasis on quality came in a speech by Henry Ford II, in November 1970, in which he predicted that all products will be increasingly designed for long, trouble-free usage rather than immediate appeal, and added that this trend is a direct result of consumer insistence.

One of the most significant ramifications of this quest for quality is that many of the traditional signs and symbols of progress and success are being challenged. The continued increase in the Gross National Product is being questioned. Economists and conservationists are demanding to know the hidden cost of this quantitative growth in terms of environmental pollution and the adverse impact on the quality of life. All across the country the budget preparation process is being revised to measure output in terms of program and performance, rather than simply to report input in terms of dollars. A college or graduate school or seminary degree no longer carries the prestige or value that it had a decade ago. Prospective employers are less impressed by the quantity of time the individual spent in an institution of higher learning and are more interested in asking qualitative questions about the person's competence.

This quest for quality is producing similar challenges to the traditional signs and symbols in the parish. Unquestionably, the most highly visible, the most controversial, and the most important of these changes in the meaning of symbols and words in the parish has been the dropping of the letter S from the word missions. As church members have become increasingly concerned about evaluating the purpose and the quality of performance of their church in terms of mission, the priorities of denominations as well as of congregations have been radically reordered. The prestige of a congregation today often is determined more by what it is doing than by its size or building.

Perhaps one of the least visible but most highly significant of these changes is in membership training. Twenty years ago, in many congregations, the emphasis was on numbers and quantity, and many new members were received with little or no preparation or training. Today in those same congregations a six- or nine- or twenty-one- or thirty-six-month confirmation class has replaced the six- or twelve-week membership class for young people. In addition all adults, including those transferring their membership from other congregations, are expected to attend a series of training sessions.

This same shift from quantity to quality can be seen in the reporting by pastors on the total membership of their congregations. In the 1950s, the dominant emphasis was on the size of the number reported to the denominational headquarters. In recent years, more and more pastors are placing the emphasis on the quality of members, rather than on the length of the membership list. The effort to make sure each number in the membership total represents a live and reasonably active member has been one of the major reasons for the leveling off in the total membership figures for such denominations as the United Presbyterian Church, The United Methodist Church, the United Church of Christ, and The Christian Church (Disciples of Christ).

One of the most highly visible and impressive areas of parish life in which this quest for quality can be seen is Christian education. While journalists have been focusing their attention on the continued quantitative decline of the Sunday school, professionals have been helping to create a variety of opportunities for personal and spiritual growth. The traditional Sunday school is only one part of the total picture, as less emphasis is being given to the number of people who attend and more concern is being expressed over what happens to the people who are present. The Sunday school also illustrates one of the interesting minor consequences of this new emphasis on quality. For decades the universal yardstick for evaluating the Sunday school was a quantitative index, the attendance figure. Now the emphasis has shifted to quality in many parishes, but the yardstick that measures quantity is still being used in the evaluation process even though many leaders in the field agree that quality does not necessarily produce quantitative gains.

This new emphasis on quality also can be seen in the growing number of congregations that are taking seriously the value of continuing self-evaluation. While statistics are still a part of this process, they no longer dominate it. Today it is not unusual to find a congregation that is planning and evaluating its program and ministry by the use of such qualitative terms as purpose, servanthood, celebration, growth, hope, and outreach.

The evangelism committee continues to report the total number of new members received each year, but it also is answering questions such as these: How many persons joined on profession of faith? How many of the new members have been assimilated into the fellowship of the congregation? What has happened in the lives of the people who have joined this fellowship? The finance committee continues to report the total receipts and the total expenditures for the year, but is also reporting how the money was used in programmatic terms. The women's auxiliary continues to report the number of meetings held during the past year, but, in addition, is expected to report what happened because these meetings were held. The Christian education committee continues to render a statistical report on participation, but the heart of its report is in the statement of its goals or aims for the year, how it developed a program to achieve those goals, and an evaluation of what happened. The pastor in these congregations may give more space in his annual accounting to the congregation to what he learned during the past year that will enable him to be a better pastor than to the statistical summary of visits, marriages, funerals, and worship services.

The ramifications of this quest for quality can be found in every segment of American society from the political arena, where mediocrity has been rejected as a qualification for a position on the United States Supreme Court, to the criteria used by middle-aged men who are considering a change in vocation.

In attempting to predict the impact of this trend on the local church, four patterns of response stand out. The first, the shift in emphasis from quantity to quality, already has been discussed.

The second is that the program, ministry, and operation of that social institution called the local church will become more complex. It is a truism among behavioral scientists that any move in the direction of becoming more sensitive to the needs of people increases the complexity of the operation. Relevant illustrations of this can be found in the evolution of the public assistance programs in the United States, in the changes in means of financing government, in the treatment of mental illnesses, in the marketing programs of automobile manufacturers, in the involvement of the churches in the civil rights movement and in antipoverty programs, and in the changes in public education during the past three decades.

The same pattern can be anticipated in every congregation that places the primary emphasis on performance rather than on size, that focuses on meeting the needs of people rather than on servicing the institution, or that evaluates its program not with questions such as "how many were present?" but rather with questions such as "what happened to or with those who were there?" As the quest for quality in responding to the needs of people continues, the life of the local church will become more complex. This includes a lower ratio of church members per professional staff person, a more specialized in-service training for laymen, a greater variety of specialized equipment and facilities, including buildings, a more elaborate organization in the local church and the denominational structure, with more people spending more time in more committee meetings, more complex demands on the pastor, and a greater utilization of outside resource persons.

The third pattern of response to this quest for quality is closely related to the second and is already visible in hundreds of congregations. It is a desire—the expression of which varies from a nostalgic longing to a militant demand—to "get back to the good old days when life was simpler." While they speak from different perspectives and with differing sets of motivations, two groups lead in this demand today for a simpler organizational operation—the fundamentalist advocates of a "back to the Bible" approach to parish and denominational life, and some of the radical renewalists.

In both cases the nostalgic desire to return to the good old days when life was simpler translates into an operational goal to be less sensitive to the needs of people and less aware of the differences among people. Betty White would have little sympathy with this desire to return to the good old days.

Finally, it should be recognized that this quest for quality is going to be filled with a tremendous quantity and variety of frustrations. As the quest continues, we will discover that being more responsive to the needs of people means having not only a more complex operation, but also a more expensive one. We will discover also that much of what we have always known about improving the quality of performance of the parish isn't true and many of the most widely acclaimed approaches don't work. The silver lining in this cloud, however, is that God is still at work in his world and the power of the Holy Spirit usually is underestimated rather than overstated.

10

Who's in Charge Here?

"I'm sorry I can't take you into our new church parlor,"
said Jack Taylor to his old college classmate Don Johnson,
"but there's only one key. The women raised the money for
this room, and bought the furnishings—and the president of our church women's organization has the only
key. If you stand over here, however, you can see part of
the inside of the room through this window. They did
a tremendous job of decorating and furnishing it, and
it's the most attractive room in the whole building."

Don had stopped by to pick up Jack and another pastor for the four-hour drive to the annual denominational
pastors' school. They had agreed to meet at Jack's and
they were taking a quick tour through the new building
before going on their way.

As they continued through the new structure, Tom
Wilson, an associate minister in the 3,300-member Calvary
Church on the other side of the city, commented with
envy, "This is a beauty of a fellowship hall! You have
less than half as many members as we have at Calvary, but
we don't have anything that can begin to compare with

this." As he looked around at the beautifully decorated, carpeted, and softly lighted, hundred-foot-long room he added, "This is just what we needed last Saturday. The daughter of one of our most active members was married in the church, but the wedding reception was held downtown in a hotel, because our fellowship hall is too small and too noisy to accommodate a large crowd. You get two or three hundred people in there all talking at once, and you can't hear yourself think, the way the noise bounces off the walls and ceilings."

"We had a big wedding reception in here shortly after we moved into the building," replied Jack Taylor, "and that ended that. It took our custodian most of a day to get the cake out of the rug. The trustees have decided that no refreshments can be served in here, so now we use that double classroom across the hall that has a folding door in the middle for any kind of group that has refreshments."

"Who did you say made that policy?" asked Tom Wilson, "the custodian or the trustees?"

"The trustees, of course," began Jack Taylor. "Oh, I see your point now. Well, to be more precise, I guess you can say the policy was initiated by the custodian and approved by the trustees."

This conversation illustrates one of the most important issues in the parish today. It is an issue that often divides laymen, frequently pits the people against the pastor, and usually causes many needless misunderstandings. It can be compressed into five words: *Who is in charge here?*

In most congregations many people give widely varying answers to that question and, even more significantly, often articulate one set of answers but are guided in their actions by another.

One method of surfacing this issue is to list on a sheet of paper eight or ten or dozen factors that appear to be the most influential in the decision-making process in that congregation. In one congregation this sheet was circulated among the twenty members of the governing body of the congregation.

Who Is in Charge Here?

You have 100 points to divide up among these factors which influence the decision-making process here at Church Street Church. Allocate the appropriate number of points to each influence or factor. Make sure they total exactly 100.

Influence	*Percentage Points*
Tradition	
The pastor	
The church school	
The Holy Spirit	
Goals	
A dozen old-timers	
Location	
The building	
Financial limitations	
The Church Council	
Size	
Other (write in)	
	———
TOTAL	100%

Each member of the governing body was given a copy of this sheet and asked to identify and weigh the importance of each factor by indicating the relative importance of each item. One layman, for example, wrote 30 percent after tradition, gave 35 percent to the influence of the pastor, 2 percent each to the Holy Spirit, goals, location, size, and a dozen old-timers, 5 percent to the building, 10 percent to the church council, and the remaining ten percentage points he assigned to financial limitations.

After each member had completed the assignment, the sheets were collected. Both the range and the average were calculated for each item, including the write-ins under "other."

In one 1,700-member, downtown congregation the results of this tabulation, using a similar form but with a slightly different set of items, looked like this when reproduced for discussion by the governing body.

Who's in Charge at First Church?

Average*	Influence	Range of Values**
8	Tradition	0 to 20
7	Building	0 to 40
14	Location	5 to 70
6	Stained-glass windows	0 to 20
2	The radio broadcast	0 to 40
1	Goals	0 to 10
9	Music and the choir	5 to 25
10	Financial limitations	0 to 70
8	Perceived needs of people	0 to 30
3	The Holy Spirit	0 to 60
7	Ten key lay leaders	0 to 30
20	The Pastor	5 to 80
5	Others (write-ins)	1 to 30

* The "average" is the arithmetic mean, arrived at by adding the total points assigned to each item and dividing by the number of papers turned in.

** The "range" simply reports the lowest and the highest number assigned to each item.

The use of this procedure in a 300-member congregation in a rural community of 4,600 residents resulted in this summary.

Who's in Charge at Grace Church?

Average	Influence	Range
4	The nature of this community	0 to 40
8	The Holy Spirit	0 to 30
12	The building	5 to 50
4	The National Football League*	0 to 20
6	The choir	2 to 17
13	Tradition	10 to 60
5	A widespread conservatism	0 to 70
26	The minister	15 to 80
7	The Sunday school	0 to 20
3	The women's organization	0 to 30
9	The lakes*	0 to 40
3	Apathy	0 to 16

This same procedure was used by a 90-member, open-country church; the responses from twenty-two leaders, including several teen-agers, are reproduced in this summary.

Who's in Charge at Oak Grove Church?

Average	Influence	Range
12	The preacher	0 to 70
38	The cemetery	5 to 60
8	The church council	5 to 15

* In this congregation, as in many others, it was openly recognized that the schedule of the televised games of the National Football League in the fall had influenced the church schedule for all day Sunday as well as for Monday evening, while the attractiveness of the nearby lakes was a major force all summer long.

Average	Influence	Range
19	Four laymen	0 to 60
18	Yesterday	0 to 80
5	The Holy Spirit	0 to 15

It is important to tailor the categories to fit each situation. This can be illustrated by comparing the categories used at Oak Grove and at St. Luke's, a 1,785-member, suburban congregation in a southern metropolitan area.

Who's in Charge at St. Luke's?

Average	Influence	Range
3	Location	0 to 15
10	Building facilities	5 to 25
3	The Bible	0 to 10
14	The heavy emphasis on program	0 to 60
5	Financial limitations	0 to 80
8	The music program	5 to 35
6	The church school schedule	0 to 62
4	The Holy Spirit	0 to 45
17	The senior minister	5 to 80
2	Traditions	0 to 10
4	The business manager	0 to 30
11	Response to human need	0 to 50
5	Goals	0 to 38
8	A lack of trust	0 to 65

In using this procedure it is helpful to prepare a list and ask everyone to work from the same list. A simple, open-ended questionnaire will provide some interesting responses, but these responses are nearly impossible to tabulate in a meaningful manner that can be used for subsequent discussion. The use of a form "depersonalizes" the responses and reduces the degree of defensiveness in any subsequent discussion.

There are several ways of building the list that will be circulated. One is to interview persons individually and use an open-ended question like "Who's in charge around here, how are decisions made, and who or what influences what this church does and how it does it?" Another way is to ask a group of people to "brainstorm" the question. A third is to analyze what has been happening and attempt to perceive why certain decisions came out the way they did. A fourth is to ask four or five people to build lists separately and then produce a composite. A fifth is to combine the first four.

This procedure has several values for the pastor and the people who want to increase the degree of intentionality in the decision-making process in their parish, to help one another understand the differences among people, or to accelerate the pace of planned change.

One of the most obvious values in this procedure is that it quickly reveals any discrepancies that may exist among the people or between a leadership group and the pastor in how they perceive the decision-making process operates. If the discrepancy is large this procedure opens up opportunities for creative discussion.

Perhaps more important is the discrepancy between the ideal and reality. While a few people will respond with idealized interpretations of the influences on the decision-making process, most people tend to be very frank and realistic in describing what they perceive to be the active forces at work. For example, only rarely do either "the Holy Spirit" or "goals" secure more than five or ten points each in the composite score from a group of fifteen or twenty parish leaders. This procedure almost automatically produces an identification of the discrepancy between "the way it is here" and "the way it ought to be here." The resulting discontent is the essential first step in planned change.[1]

A third value in the use of this simple procedure is that it enables people, and especially a new pastor, to gain very quickly an idea of how others see the local situation and of the reality with which he is confronted.

This procedure is also a very helpful tool for the layman or minister who is consciously interested in the question of leadership style. By including four or five items such as "the pastor," "a small group of very influential laymen," "the church council," "properly elected and designated leaders," "three families," or "the pastor and two or three of his very close allies" it is possible to discover what people *believe* to be the current style or pattern of leadership in the parish. What people believe to be reality, rather than reality itself, often is the best beginning point for planning changes.

If the parish has both a program-planning committee or council and a separate administrative board it may be helpful to ask each group to participate separately in this exercise, and then to compare the composite scores for the two groups. Occasionally this is very revealing.

Finally, this procedure is one of the doors that can lead to a creative discussion of purpose, of the reason for the existence of *this* parish, and of the distinction between ends (goals) and the means to an end.

---

[1] For an elaboration on the place of discontent in the process of planned change see Lyle E. Schaller, *The Local Church Looks to the Future* (Nashville: Abingdon Press, 1968), pp. 225-27 or Schaller, *The Change Agent*, pp. 89-96, 122-23.

11

Reading
The Election Returns

"Today every pastor should be an expert in reading the election returns," advised John J. McCoy, Ph.D., a professor of political science at the state university, and a member of the church council at St. John's. "A lot of you ministers don't like to think in these terms, but a parish resembles a political operation in many respects," continued Professor McCoy. "One of the reasons we have had so many petty little problems here at St. John's during the past decade is that our membership includes so many pietists who believe in neither the doctrine of original sin nor the rule of reciprocity."

"I believe I know a little about the doctrine of original sin," responded Pastor Don Johnson, "but I'm not sure I understand what you mean by reading the election returns or the rule of reciprocity." Don and his wife had been invited to the McCoys' for dinner, and now Don and Professor McCoy were relaxing in the living room. Don had been looking forward to the opportunity to get better acquainted with this parishioner, who at forty-two was a very active leader at St. John's, in his third term on the city commission, a member of the executive committee of the state Democratic Party, and the author of three books on American government.

"Let's look at these one at a time," replied Professor McCoy. "Here at St. John's we conduct a couple hundred elections every year. Call them referenda, if you want to be precise, but in each case we ask people to vote.

"The most obvious are the referenda we conduct every Sunday morning. First, everyone votes on the question 'Do I go to worship at St. John's this morning?' Next we each vote on the question, 'How much financial support does St. John's deserve from me?' We have a third vote. 'Should I go to Sunday school today or not?' Now if you count just those three questions, that means 156 votes a year. If you add in all the other meetings, programs, fund-raising drives, special events, and other occasions when people are asked to say yes or no, we must take at least 300 votes a year here at St. John's. Now, my question is this, Don, who is studying and interpreting the returns from all of those elections?"

"I'm afraid I have some problems in placing the preaching of the word and the administration of the sacraments in the same category with electing someone to the city commission," replied Don Johnson. "I'm afraid I can't quite equate a person's response to his membership vows with a vote on a school bond issue."

"You're missing the point, Pastor," continued Professor McCoy. "It's not a matter of developing categories that make you comfortable. The only choice you have is whether or not you're going to try to interpret what people are saying when they attend church or stay away or when they raise or cut their giving. Every politician will agree that people send you a message in their actions. **You can't** control the sending of those messages. A wise leader, however, will try to understand the message that is being sent. He may not agree with it, but he'll try to identify it."

"In the church, however, so many people want to put their heads in the sand like an ostrich and pretend no messages are being sent. I've argued with people at St. John's on this for years. I say that if someone who ordinarily is in church nearly every Sunday misses three weeks in a row, you'd better assume he is sending a message and try to figure out what it is. Now maybe he's been in Florida for a vacation, and there's no distress signal there; but he's still asking, 'Did you miss me while I was gone?' Likewise, if a person's not been in church for six months and all of a sudden he's at worship two or three Sundays in a row, you'd better assume he's sending you a message."

"Now I'm beginning to see what you mean," replied Pastor Johnson, "but what do you suggest we do?"

"Well, first of all, we have to believe that election returns should be interpreted," continued Professor McCoy with some satisfaction, as he saw he was beginning to win a convert. "As nearly as I can figure out, the policy at St. John's is to pretend we don't have any elections, so no one has to interpret the result of the voting."

"All right, let's assume you have convinced me we have a lot of different votes at St. John's every month," interrupted Don, with a smile; "you still haven't told me how to interpret what they tell me."

"You have at least four choices on that," replied Dr. McCoy glibly. "You can ignore them as we have been doing for years at St. John's. You can interpret them by yourself and attempt to impose your unilateral interpretation on the rest of the congregation. You can sit down with a number of the leaders at St. John's and try to figure out what the votes mean. Or you can go out and listen to the people as they explain why they voted as they did. This fourth alternative is what the pollsters and the politicians do, and I'm convinced they are more skillful at reading election returns than most church leaders."

"Now let's translate all of this into simple language for a simple preacher," said Don. "What are you suggesting we should do? Go out and ask people why they missed church or why they came and why they put the amount of money they did in the offering plate?"

"You could do worse," came the response from the political scientist. "What I actually suggested was to go out and listen to the people. There's a vast difference between asking questions and listening. My advice would be to do as little talking as possible and a lot more listening. I don't see anything to prevent forty people from this parish going out and making five listening calls each. That would cover two hundred households plus the forty they represent. That's almost the whole congregation, isn't it?"

"Not quite," replied Don. "We have 312 households represented on our parish membership roll. But that's not my concern. I still am not sure what these people say when they go to call. What kind of questions are they instructed to ask?"

"They don't ask questions, they listen! They don't go in with a long list of questions," replied Professor McCoy. "They go in with only one question, and that's 'How are things going with you?' They may have to learn how to ask this in eight different ways, but they go to listen, not to cross-examine."

"I guess I understand what you're saying, but now let's take up the rule of reciprocity you mentioned earlier," said Don who appeared ready to change the subject.

"You may have heard this described in political language as 'you scratch my back and I'll scratch yours,'" responded Don's host. "What it means basically is that when someone does you a favor, it helps the interpersonal relationships if you return the favor. It may sound rather crass, but if you take the doctrine of original sin seriously you can understand it. My problem is that I find so few clergymen who are able to think in political terms, and they don't understand the relevance of these concepts."

"Now that you've explained it I think I know what you're talking about," replied Don, as he thought of his own suggestion for recognizing the contributions of volunteer workers at St. John's and of the carefully prepared displays his Presbyterian neighbor provided in response to growth in the attendance when the session meetings were moved into the church parlor.

"There are two more political terms that a minister might do well to keep in mind," continued Prof. McCoy. "The first is service your clientele. A good Congressman is very careful to respond to all the requests he gets from his constituency. By contrast I am amazed at how often I hear a layman complain because he wrote a letter to his church or to a denominational office and never got a reply." As he heard this, Don smiled and thought about James Glasse's admonition to ministers to pay their rent promptly.

"The last point I want to make concerns the many political decisions that have to be made in the church," explained Dr. McCoy. "I know most of our people at St. John's think that politics is a dirty business, but every decision that allocates a scarce resource is a political decision. It doesn't matter whether you're talking about the location of the municipal swimming pool, how much of the church budget goes for benevolences, the decision to build a new interstate highway, how much of your time you will spend calling in homes, the level of Social Security payments, or whether Joe Doakes will agree to teach Sunday school rather than serve as a trustee. In each case you're talking about the allocation of scarce resources and those are political decisions."

"Maybe we should ask you to make that speech to our finance committee here at St. John's," smiled Pastor Johnson. "In a few months they'll be forced to make some tough political decisions about next year's budget."

"They'll do a better job if they realize that they are making political decisions," contended Prof. McCoy. "I think the basic reason St. John's is in a financial squeeze right now is because we haven't been very alert in reading the political signs. You've been around here long enough now, Pastor, to know that the leveling off in the giving here at St. John's is a political issue, not a result of economic conditions. We have a lot of people on the finance committee who prefer to hide behind an explanation tied to the economic conditions in this area, but in their hearts they know it's a political problem."

When Don and his wife left the McCoys that night, Mrs. Johnson commented, "Dr. McCoy is a very nice person, but he's kind of a nut about politics, isn't he? Mrs. McCoy and I couldn't help overhearing the lecture he delivered to you while we were doing the dishes. She and I both thought it awful to compare the ministry of the church with a political organization."

"Some people may get a little upset over the terminology, but what really struck me is that as he talked about the political dimensions of church administration I discovered that I have been far more conscious of political considerations than I ever realized. To put it in Professor McCoy's terminology, you may have married an ecclesiastical politician—and neither of us realized it until tonight."

Later as he reflected on the lesson in practical church politics that he had received that evening, Don began to see additional similarities between his role as a pastor and the style of the effective political leader.

One of the characteristics of the political scene that disturbs many expert observers is that frequently people vote for an individual rather than for the issues or for the party; Dwight Eisenhower was re-elected President of the United States along with the election of a Democratic House and Senate in 1956. This was the first time in over a century that a President from one party was elected at the same time that both houses of Congress went to the other party. Some contend that the country wanted a "pastor," and President Eisenhower was an outstanding pastoral type leader.

In the parish many of the most effective pastors are not great preachers or outstanding administrators or learned scholars; they are ministers who love people and who have a gift of being able to relate to people.

Don also reflected on such subjective characteristics as a sense of timing, being able to feel the mood of the people, mastery of the art of persuasion, credibility and trust, a tolerance of differences on issues without personalizing those differences, and the widely used term *charisma*. None of these is uncommon among outstanding political leaders. None is uncommon among outstanding pastors.

Perhaps, thought Don to himself, the effective pastor, like the effective politician, should cultivate a skill at reading the election returns.

123

12

Assumptions
in Church Finances

"Many of the problems we have in the church are caused by the fact that ministers tend to speak Greek and most people understand only Hebrew," commented a Lutheran pastor. He was explaining a poster-covered wall in the narthex of his church to Don Johnson, Bob Smith, and Everett Wright, who were spending a Thursday morning visiting two other pastors in the metropolitan area.

"Greek is a language that lends itself to the communication of abstract concepts. Hebrew is a 'picture' language. In Hebrew the speaker draws word pictures the listener can visualize in his mind," continued the Lutheran minister.

"We used to have our benevolence treasurer prepare a monthly financial report for our members showing the goals we had set for ourselves and the amount of money that had been received for each of the several categories. Eventually we realized this was in Greek, and no one really understood it. Here, as in every other parish I have seen, the people understand only Hebrew.

"Two years ago we began a completely different approach and translated our benevolence treasurer's report into Hebrew. You can see it here on this wall," he said pointing to a thirty-foot-long, concrete-block wall in the narthex. Beginning about three feet above the floor and running along the entire wall in three tiers was a series of posters. Each one of these ninety sheets of poster board described one of the ministries this congregation was helping to support through its benevolence giving.

One sheet had a picture of a Lutheran college pasted on it with the figure $685 written below it. Another, the picture of a tape recorder priced at $200, which this church had agreed to provide for a mission school in Hong Kong. A third depicted an inner city church and below it was indicated the amount this parish was contributing to that work. A fourth had a picture of a former pastor, now retired, and below it was written the amount this congregation was paying to retired ministers and minister's widows through the denominational apportionment for pensions.

"We finance most of these through the parish budget," continued the minister, "but nearly half are picked up by individuals, families, and groups within the congregation such as church school classes, the women's organization, the men's fellowship, and the youth group."

On this sunny October morning nearly seventy of the posters had a large black X drawn across them.

"What do all of the big X's mean?" inquired Everett Wright.

The pastor explained, "Whenever the treasurer has in hand all the money for any one item shown here, he uses a black marker to draw a big X across the poster. That way everyone knows that particular benevolence item has been completely paid. In this way we keep an up-to-date report of our benevolence record before the people at all times. Whenever one of our members walks through here he gets an up-to-date report from the benevolence treasurer—in Hebrew."

This is the way this parish has changed from a dull abstract style to a colorful illustrative one in presenting the report of the benevolence treasurer to the members.

This incident also illustrates one of the basic assumptions that merits consideration by parish leaders as they evaluate the results of their efforts to provide the necessary base for the church's ministry and program. It is apparent that the assumptions on which the financial program is developed are important in determining the success or failure of the financial effort.

This point interested Don, Bob, and Everett the most. They knew when Don had agreed to come to St. John's Church several months ago that something would have to be done about the church's finances. Total receipts at St. John's had climbed from $41,200 to $51,600 in three years and then had leveled off at approximately $51,000 for three years in a row. The three men had agreed something would have to be done to get the parish off this financial plateau. They felt that the increase in worship attendance the last several months ultimately would have a favorable impact on the total giving. They also were impressed with the strong views of Dr. Frank Harris at First Presbyterian that there was a proper place for well-publicized special offerings for designated mission work several times a year.

All three of these leaders from St. John's were still uncomfortable, however, with their own level of competence in the area of church finances. So when Don heard about the high level of giving of this Lutheran parish, he had called the pastor for an appointment.

What basic assumptions proved helpful to the leaders at St. John's when they got around to taking a serious look at the finances of the parish? Below is a copy of the list that Don and four of his laymen finally put together for consideration by the finance committee at St. John's.

1. Most church members understand Hebrew (pictures), so do not use Greek (abstractions) to communicate with them.

This point was explained by the Lutheran pastor. When you ask for pledges, present the budget in terms of needs your members understand. Likewise, when you report to the congregation on the finances of the congregation, translate the report into items and services and needs that speak to people.

2. People who appear to be apathetic or inactive or disinterested have reasons for this attitude. One way to approach such persons is by exhortation. A better approach is by listening.

It matters little whether one is talking about evangelism, a new ministry to the community, an effort to induce members to pledge to the church budget, or increasing attendance at Sunday morning worship, the only place to begin the conversation is with the other person's agenda.

For years church leaders have approached inactive members with exhortations and suggestions about what they should do to support their church. The overall results have been discouraging. A more realistic approach is to begin on the assumption that a person has reasons for his actions and attitudes and the appropriate starting point for the church visitor is to listen to these reasons.

3. The giving level in a local church tends to reflect each member's perception of need, the quality of internal communication, and the degree of the member's involvement in the life, program, and ministry of that congregation far more than it reflects the financial capability or the commitment or the loyalty of each member.

Traditionally, the cry of frustrated leaders in the local church has been, "If our people were only more committed—"; or "If the people today were as loyal as they used to be, we would have no trouble financing our church program"; or "If you people had more money we could finance more of the things we should be doing."

A careful analysis of the experience of many congregations indicates that a more important variable is how well the members perceive the needs. This point was underscored repeatedly in the North American Interchurch Study. The members' perception of needs tends to be dependent on how closely they are related to the ongoing life of the parish or the quality (not quantity) of information going from the parish to the membership.

4. People will respond to real needs when they become aware of them.

Closely related to the previous point is the assumption that people will respond when they become aware of needs. In one tiny congregation with a $5,500 annual budget the furnace broke down in January and the plumbing froze. Within two weeks the people had raised $4,800 to replace the furnace and repair the damage. In another parish a well-known, local young couple entered the foreign mission field and the congregation tripled its total benevolence giving. In a third, receipts doubled the year after the congregation undertook a large building program. In each case the need was clearly perceived by everyone. Dr. Frank Harris' experiences at First Presbyterian Church (see chapter 8) are other examples of this same point.

5. The "loyalty button" is out of order.

Only a few years ago people would contribute to the work of the church simply out of loyalty. Today they want to know how the money will be used. Yesterday it was possible to say "this goes with the franchise. If you hang a sign that says United Methodist on the building, there are certain obligations that go with the right to use that label. This is one of them." Today people want to know why a cause is considered meritorious, and they want to know how the money will be used. The credibility gap has widened significantly all across society, and the institutional expression of the church is no exception to this generalization. People quite properly believe they have a right to know and they do not wish to simply rely on the judgment of a handful of distant leaders, many of whom they do not know.

6. Interpersonal relationships have a tremendous influence on the quality of communication among people.

If a person stops and asks directions while driving along the highway or in a strange city, does he feel more confident about the accuracy of what he is told when he receives advice from a friend or from a total stranger? Think about this when choosing the people to make calls in the next every member canvass.

7. Two-way communication is superior to one-way communication.

This is self-evident. Many times we choose to go see someone or to talk to someone on the telephone rather than simply to send a letter. We intuitively know this will improve the quality of our communication.

Therefore, why expect to finance the church budget simply by sending out letters? Perhaps some people feel the only effective way they have left to respond to a letter asking for money is to make no response.

8. The quality and volume of the competition in communicating to people has been rising very rapidly in recent years.

Perhaps the clearest evidence of this trend is that since 1964 giving to charitable and philanthropic causes has been increasing at a much faster rate than giving to churches. In the inflationary era of 1950-55, the trend was just the opposite.

9. In communicating with people about church finances, begin with their needs, not with trying to encourage them to feel an interest in solving your problem.

There is an axiom in marketing that the organization that concentrates on "pushing its product" tends to go out of business, while the one that concentrates on meeting the needs of people tends to open the door to innovation and new possibilities.[1] That also applies to your church.

10. There are at least three points of "financial pain" being felt in the churches today. One is felt by the people responsible for program planning and implementation in the local church. A second is felt by the persons responsible for administration of the work of the local church. A third is felt by those in denominational and interdenominational agencies.

Closely related to the previous point is this third assumption. If you take the first two seriously, then any

[1] Theodore Levitt, *Innovation in Marketing* (New York: McGraw-Hill Book Co., 1962). This is an exceptionally perceptive book about the relationships between an organization and its clientele.

effort to finance the budget of a denominational or inter-denominational agency must begin by looking at and responding to the first of these three points of "financial pain."

11. The longer a local church delays the beginning of planning for its finances, the fewer the options open and the lower the chances of a satisfactory outcome from the planning efforts.

If this assumption is correct, the time to begin planning for next year's every member canvass is immediately on the conclusion of this year's efforts. The longer this is delayed, the fewer the options open for next year.

12. Any program or effective effort in this area is limited by the traditions, values, attitudes, and practices of each local church. Unless this is recognized, there is a limit on what a training program for individuals in the church can accomplish.

Precedent and tradition are the strongest forces in the making of nearly every decision, from where you will sit at the table when you eat with your family to where you sit in church or how much you will give to support your parish next year.

Precedent and tradition will determine the ceiling on the local budget, *unless a careful effort is made to replace the old traditions and precedents with new ones.*

As Don, Bob, Everett, and the other members of the finance committee reflected on this list of assumptions they came up with three decisions.

First, they decided to ask Prof. John McCoy, the political expert in the congregation, to give them some help in reading the election returns. They began to see that the three-year leveling off in total receipts did resemble votes cast in an election, and that maybe they should try to interpret the message that was being sent by a significant number of the members at St. John's.

Second, they decided to reduce the volume of printed and mimeographed material they would use in their financial campaign and to increase the volume of person-to-person, two-way communication.[2]

Third, they decided that, beginning this year, they would use Hebrew rather than Greek in communicating to the membership about the program, ministry, outreach, and finances of St. John's.

---

[2] For an introduction to one method of increasing the value of person-to-person contacts see Schaller, *Parish Planning*, pp. 56-63.

13

Turning People Loose

"Daddy, Daddy, come here and see what's happening," called Pastor Johnson's ten-year-old daughter, Laura, with great excitement in her voice. It was the second day after the Johnsons had moved into the parsonage two blocks down the street from St. John's Church. Their two daughters, Becky and Laura, shared a second-floor bedroom, and as Laura led her father into the bedroom she pointed out the window to a tall evergreen growing next to the house. By getting into the proper position Don could look out the window and see down into a nest with three robin's eggs in it. "We'll be able to watch the eggs hatch and see the baby robins grow," squealed Laura with great delight.

For several weeks the Johnsons had a spectacular view of Mr. and Mrs. Robin's efforts to raise a new family. It was a great day when the eggs finally hatched and they saw the three, tiny, baby robins. The Johnsons watched as the parents worked harder and harder to feed the three rapidly growing and apparently ever hungry babies. In a few short weeks the baby birds were so large they began to overflow the nest.

One Saturday afternoon Mr. and Mrs. Robin apparently had decided the time had come for the babies to leave the nest. They encouraged the most venturesome to stand on the edge of the nest; after several minutes of watching his father flying around, he plunged off on his own wobbly flight. After landing on a lower branch of a nearby tree he took off again and soon flew up into a tree across the street. Next the mother and father robin came back and coaxed their second offspring to test his wings. An hour later they were back, and the last of the three, fat, young robins flew out of the nest. By late afternoon the nest that had been overflowing with hungry young robins a few hours earlier was empty.

The experience of this family of robins has been repeated every year for centuries and illustrates one of the most significant trends in contemporary American society —the move away from the structures that contain us. This trend will have a major impact on the churches in the coming years, just as it had a major impact on Don Johnson's ministry at St. John's Church.

The Shift Away from Confinement

For decades the pattern in the United States has been to confine people in buildings. Now this pattern is being reversed, and the current emphasis is on getting people out of the array of cages, boxes, nests, rooms, and buildings in which they have been encouraged to cluster.

This trend can be seen in the decreased time the typical patient spends in a hospital. The operation that required a stay of from seven to ten days in the hospital in 1940 now finds the patient leaving the hospital after only three or four days.

The orphanages that flourished in the half century following the Civil War have been almost completely replaced by publicly financed programs that enable the children to live in the home of a relative or in foster homes.

This same trend can be seen in the lessening number of persons in institutions for the mentally ill and mentally retarded. The number of persons in these institutions increased annually until 1967 and 1968, when, with the greater emphasis on outpatient care and the use of community mental health centers, the number began to decrease. Today the emphasis in the care of the mentally ill is not to confine them in buildings, but to get them out of institutions.

The old pattern of a child going to a school building and staying in his assigned room for the entire school day is being altered with the emergence of the "open classroom," the school without walls, and the emphasis on experienced learning that is sharply increasing the hours spent outside the traditional classroom.

Hundreds of colleges and universities now expect the student to spend a semester or a year off campus, often abroad, rather than to follow the traditional pattern of four years on the same campus. A growing number of schools now offer a home study program that enables a person to obtain a college degree without ever attending any classes on campus.

The relatively sudden emergence of this trend has caused severe financial problems for scores of colleges and universities that borrowed money to build dormitories for the anticipated increase in the student enrollment; for now these building are only partially filled as a growing proportion of students are electing to live off campus.

One of the most significant examples of this trend is reflected in the prison population of the nation. For decades the number of persons in federal and state prisons was approximately equal to one-tenth of one percent of the total population of the country. As the population grew, the prison population rose. The year 1966, however, marked a reversal of this trend, and the past half dozen years have seen a sharp decline in the number of persons in prison. During a recent three-year period, for example, the prison population in the state of California declined by approximately one-third.

Another evidence of the growth of this basic trend is the change in the behavior pattern of the unwed mother. Five years ago most homes for unwed mothers were filled to capacity and many had a waiting list. Today nearly half of them have closed or have changed their function, and many others are facing the possibility of closing for lack of clients, despite a continued increase in illegitimate births. The typical, pregnant, seventeen-year-old high school girl today, instead of being sent away to spend several months in a maternity home in another city, is continuing in school and expects to raise her baby at home.

This move away from confining people to buildings can be seen in many other segments of society. For thirty years the pattern was to build large concentrations of public housing units to house the poor of the cities. The Housing Act of 1968 reversed this pattern. The "ribbon" shopping center of the 1950s, consisting of a series of boxlike stores facing the highway with the parking lot in front, has been replaced by the enclosed and air-conditioned mall that greatly increases the sense of freedom of the shopper. The bank with its series of metal cages and little offices of the 1930s has been replaced by an open floor plan with a dozen or more officers' desks in a living-room type environment. All across the country zoos are being rebuilt to get animals out of the barns and cages and into an environment resembling their native habitat.

What Has Been the Impact on the Churches?

In looking at this trend in an attempt to discover the implications for the churches it may be helpful first to look quickly at three "snapshots" of the church in America and at what is happening in thousands of congregations.

The first picture shows the type of church architecture that has become known as the Akron plan. This style flourished in the half century between 1875 and 1925 and included a series of tiny cubicles for Sunday school classes running along two or three sides of a larger assembly hall.

The second shows the eight- or twelve- or sixteen-room, two-story, "Sunday school wing" that was added on to an existing structure between 1948 and 1968.

The third snapshot shows the cavernous, often dark and gloomy nave that provides seats for eight hundred or a thousand persons at worship. (Today the typical attendance at any one service seldom exceeds two or three hundred.)

Each of these three pictures presents a structure that was planned and built on the same principle that was the basis for the construction of thousands of hospitals, prisons, orphanages, schools, college dormitories, strip shopping centers, public housing towers, banks, and zoos. In each case there was an implicit assumption that people would be assigned rooms and would stay in their assigned rooms for specified periods of time.

While each individual's own value system will influence his choice of words in describing what has happened, the basic pattern is that increasingly the trend is away from assigning people to rooms for specified periods of time. The boxes have been opened. The nests are being emptied. We are beginning to move away from the practice of confining people to rooms.

In the church school the trend toward intergenerational classes, experienced learning, the three- or four-hour, one-day-a-week, after-school program, and field trip experiences has left many parishes with an excess of traditional classrooms.

Likewise the trend toward two or three or four worship services made the large sanctuary with the overhanging balcony functionally obsolete and excessively expensive to maintain. Similarly, many of the bowling alleys and gymnasiums that were a part of so many church buildings erected in the first half of this century are now seldom used, as the fellowship activities of the congregation no longer are confined to the church building.

What Are the Implications for Tomorrow?

In reflecting on this trend we find rising to the surface four points that Don Johnson concluded should be brought to the attention of the parish at St. John's.

The first is the requirement for a new approach to planning church buildings. In the past most church buildings have been designed to satisfy such statements as "Design us a building that will accommodate 250 at worship and provide twelve Sunday school rooms"; or "Here is the program we have projected for our parish for the next decade; design a building that will house that program."

Each of these statements carries with it the assumption that in the future people can be managed as they have been managed in the past and that they should *and* will go to the assigned rooms at the specified time.

Today perhaps the clearest instruction that a parish building committee can offer an architect is "We don't know what in the way of program this congregation will want or need to house ten years from now. Design a building that we can build today, pay for in no more than seven or eight years, and find sufficiently flexible not only to accommodate our present program, but also to house whatever the leaders in this congregation a decade from now see as the appropriate response to the needs of the people."

While this may sound unusually vague, here and there church buildings are being constructed on the dual premise that it is possible to house today's program and also to maximize the options that will be open to parish leaders in 1980 and 1985.

A second implication of this trend toward reducing the control of buildings over people is already being heard in many congregations. A typical statement is "We're spending 40 percent of our budget on the building. That's more than we allocate to benevolences or spend on ministry to people."

A traditional response to this complaint has been, "But you don't understand! Maintaining this building is a part of our ministry to our members and also a part of our mission in this community."

The trend away from confining people to buildings is

increasing. A number of people, especially younger adults, find this traditional answer to be an unsatisfactory response. One result is that a growing number of congregations are developing a budget format that uses person-centered terminology rather than the traditional, object-oriented categories in deciding the priorities for allocating the financial resources of the parish.

A far more important implication is the impact of this trend on program planning. This can be illustrated by the changing response to the frequently heard complaint "Look at all these empty rooms! Twenty years ago we had 300 in our Sunday school every week and all these rooms were filled to capacity. Now half of them are completely empty every Sunday."

A common response to this statement has been to develop new approaches for attracting neighborhood residents to attend Sunday school and thus fill up those empty rooms.

This type of program planning *begins* with the resources of the parish—in this case, some unused rooms—and moves from that point to an attempt to influence the behavior patterns of people so the resources will be utilized.

The growing visibility of the national current trend toward freeing people from confinement to rooms suggests the bankruptcy of beginning the program-planning process with an analysis of the parish's physical resources. It is becoming increasingly apparent that a more creative approach is *to begin with the needs of people* and attempt to manage the resources to meet those needs.

This leads to the fourth implication of this trend—and may also suggest *why* this trend has become so pronounced in so many different segments of society. The persons responsible for the administration of any physical facility tend to operate it primarily for the benefit and convenience of those in control and to protect the facility, rather than to operate it primarily for the benefit of the clientele it was constructed to serve. This tendency can be observed in the administration of schools, playgrounds, hospitals, prisons, public housing projects, children's homes, and countless other institutions. Very easily the means to an end can become an end in itself, preservation of the property can become more important than the use of the facility, and the nest can become a cage.

When Mr. and Mrs. Robin were encouraging their three little robins to fly out of the nest, they were illustrating a significant, contemporary trend—and they also were teaching a lesson in planning for ministry in our churches.

It also happened that Mr. and Mrs. Robin brought this lesson home to Don Johnson at a very appropriate time at St. John's. The same spring the Johnsons watched their robins grow, Mrs. Warden began what turned out to be a three- or four-year process of changing the value system on which the church school at St. John's had been built.

14

Changing the Value System

The next to last question asked of the nineteen children in the kindergarten class at St. John's Church before the end of the ninety-minute church school period was "All right now, class, who sponsored today's lesson?"

With one voice all nineteen youngsters responded, "Matthew, Mark, and Luke, the Synoptic Gospels."

If in your church school you do not teach the concept of the Synoptic Gospels until second or third grade or later, this may be something of a shock to you.

It all began when Mrs. Warden, a fifty-three-year-old woman, was asked to teach the kindergarten class at St. John's. She had not taught in the church school for over twenty years, and she felt she needed to learn more about today's five- and six-year-olds before she actually began to teach. Out of her reading, questioning, and reflections she came up with a list of sixteen guidelines that influenced her teaching. Two are relevant to this account.

She asked herself the question "What's the world like for a five- or six-year-old today?" One of her conclusions was that for children today the continuity of life is interrupted every five or ten minutes by a commercial.

She also learned from her reading that psychologists have concluded that a person's capability to remember content or factual material peaks at about age three or four or five. By the time the typical human being celebrates his sixth birthday he is firmly established on a downward curve that eventually is described with the word *senility*. (That is the reassuring thought for the day for all who have read this far.)

Mrs. Warden was firmly convinced that it is good for people to know something about the Bible, and, since kindergartners are near the peak years in their capability to remember what they learn, she decided that one of her goals would be to help these five- and six-year-olds learn not only the names of the books of the Bible, but also some of the basic teachings in the various books.

While Mrs. Warden was preparing for her new assignment, the leaders of the church school were confronted with another crisis. According to local legend the seventh-grade class was the most unruly, belligerent, obstreperous class in the history of the church. In early June the seventh-grade teacher threw up her hands in despair, surrendered, and fled the scene. Her experiences did not rank among the best-kept secrets at St. John's, and the church school leaders found themselves with September coming closer every day and no "volunteer" to teach what would be the eighth-grade class that fall.

During that same summer, Mrs. Warden happened to get acquainted with Jack Barker, a twenty-seven-year-old, junior-high-school English teacher, who had moved to the community a year earlier and who also was a member of St. John's. After considerable discussion the two of them decided that, if the Christian Education Committee would approve their proposal for "team teaching," Jack would offer to teach the eighth-grade class beginning in September.

When they met with the committee at the August meeting, Mrs. Warden introduced their proposal by saying, "Mr. Barker and I have been talking about the Sunday school and have developed what we believe is a creative and exciting plan. If you approve our plan Jack will volunteer to teach the eighth-grade class while I go ahead as we agreed with the kindergarten class."

After deliberating on this opening sentence for two or three seconds, the committee responded, "Don't bother to take time going into the details of your plan. If Mr. Barker is offering to take on the eighth-grade class this fall, we accept. We had about given up on finding anyone, and to have a man who is a professional teacher walk in and volunteer is at least a medium-sized miracle! What that bunch needs is a man who can keep order and maintain discipline, Mr. Barker, and you should be able to do that. We are deeply grateful to you for coming to our rescue. Whatever you and Mrs. Warden want to work out between the two of you has our approval. Now we have some other business to settle before we can go home. Thanks again for solving our biggest problem!"

When stripped of many of its refinements, the plan Mrs. Warden and Mr. Barker had developed was that both the kindergartners and the eighth graders would concentrate on studying the Bible during the coming year. Each class would begin with Genesis and work right through to the end, but the eighth graders would always be two weeks ahead of the kindergartners. By grouping together related books they worked out a schedule whereby they could cover the entire Bible in thirty-nine Sundays.

The heart of the plan was that the eighth graders would

pick a few of the dominant ideas or insights from each book or group of books and prepare "commercials" that would illustrate these ideas and insights in a manner which would be meaningful to kindergartners. Thus it worked out that on the second Sunday of January the kindergartners would be studying, as one unit, the first three books of the New Testament, while the eighth graders would be searching out the major incidents and themes in Acts and working in teams of two or three to prepare twenty commercials to illustrate these. While they were doing this a few eighth graders would leave the room every five or ten minutes and go down the hall to show the kindergartners one or more of the commercials about the first three gospels, which they had prepared two weeks earlier.

One of these was a very large cardboard packing box with a picture of an eye covering one side of the box. The box "walked" into the kindergarten room over the heads of three eighth-grade boys, one of whom was labeled Matthew, a second Mark, and the third Luke. All three boys looked out at the kindergartners through the cut-out pupil of the large eye painted on the box. They showed several slides, which, with the narration by "Mark," explained how these three gospel writers looked at the life and ministry of Jesus from the same perspective.

Since all the commercials were prepared two weeks before they were to be shown, Mrs. Warden had time to examine them, plan the sequence and timing, and also build in a twenty-minute period that would be free of commercials. This two-week margin also gave her time to plan her sessions around the content of the commercials.

When the pastor was asked what he thought of this arrangement, his initial response was "This is the first time in my fourteen years in the ministry I've ever had eighth graders complaining to me about ninety minutes not being long enough for Sunday school.

"The other day after school," he continued, "three of the boys came in to see me and asked, 'Say, Rev, what do you have on Romans? Because of the way you folks run this place, we only have an hour and a half on Sunday morning for class, and that's not enough time to study some of these books in the Bible, figure out what they say, and get this into form for commercials. We've been trying to work ahead, and you know, Rev, Romans is really a tough book. What do you have here in your study that'll help us find the handle on this so we can pick out some themes that will interest those little kids in the kindergarten class?'

"I loaned them a couple of commentaries on Romans plus an introduction to the New Testament, and I have a hunch they'll come up with some very interesting commercials on Romans.

"I guess the only reservation I have is in regard to the person who will be teaching these kids next year in the ninth-grade class," he concluded. "We have talked about this with the kids and with the ninth-grade teacher. Currently our plan is to have the ninth graders next year to write the curriculum for two of the adult classes. In the fall they will prepare the curriculum for the Christian Home Class, and a team of them will teach that class in the winter quarter, using the materials prepared in the fall. In the winter the rest of the class will prepare the curriculum for the Theoquests and a different team will teach the Theoquests in the spring quarter.

"We're not sure about the spring quarter," continued Pastor Johnson, "but watching those robins last spring has convinced me we can't plan to keep these kids locked up here in the church school all the time they're in high school. If we try it our eleventh- and twelfth-grade rooms will be as empty as that robins' nest was by Saturday night last spring."

While it was not a conscious and carefully planned conspiracy, what actually happened was that a coalition of a couple of robins and several people, a fifty-three-year-old grandmother, a twenty-seven-year-old junior-high-school teacher, an open-minded pastor, and a group of active and uninhibited eighth graders, had begun the process of replacing some of the traditional values in the church school at St. John's with a new value system.

When Mrs. Warden and Mr. Barker had met with the Christian Education Committee the first time the previous summer, it was very clear that the dominant values underlying the goals of the committee could be expressed in words like *discipline, order, quiet,* and *respect.*

And it was assumed that the basic pedagogical model or style for the church school was the same teacher-centered model that had been used from the beginnings of St. John's Church nearly a quarter of a century earlier.

In addition it was simply assumed that the Christian educational experiences for these eighth graders would occur in the eighth-grade room between 9:00 and 10:30 every Sunday morning.

The unlikely coalition identified earlier began the process of replacing the old value system that had undergirded the Christian education program at St. John's with a new one. The new one stressed experiential learning, the use of contemporary methods of communication, additional motivational factors, the role of the teacher as an enabling agent in the learning process, order as a means to an end and not the end itself, the extending of the educational process through the week, the freeing of people from confinement to rooms, and the nurture of creativity and innovation among potentially creative and innovative people.

As the value system in the Christian education program changed at St. John's the door was opened to the introduction of additional new models in the church school.

Before discussing some of the new models, however, it is necessary to return to Mrs. Warden's classroom to hear the last question she asked of her kindergarten class that morning they studied the synoptic gospels.

"Now, can you tell our visitor who will be sponsoring our lesson next Sunday?"

Again with one voice these nineteen youngsters called out, "The Gospel of John."

Now how did these children know that the Gospel of John followed Matthew, Mark, and Luke in the Bible? Mrs. Warden had not mentioned this in any way at all.

Each Sunday, however, for the preceding four months she had closed the class period with this same question. This was consistent with another of the sixteen points in her set of guidelines; questions asked *in advance* influence performance. After a few weeks all of the kindergartners knew that that question was going to be asked. Thus, as they came on the Sunday they were going to be studying Malachi, they had a natural inclination to want to be prepared for that final question of the morning, and this typically led them to ask, "Daddy, what comes in the Bible after Malachi?"

This was but one more way in which Mrs. Warden helped change the value system at St. John's and helped create new patterns of motivation.

15

Building Variety
into the Church School

"Pastor Johnson, I feel kind of funny asking this, but could you suggest to our son, Dave, and to his buddy, Mark Schroeder, that it would be all right if they missed Sunday school this week?"

"I'm afraid I don't understand," said a puzzled Pastor Johnson, in response to this unusual telephone request that came about a year after his arrival at St. John's Church.

"Well, you know this new Sunday school class for seventh graders that was started last fall has been a tremendous success and has produced a deep sense of loyalty among the kids," came the reply over the telephone.

"Yes, I know it is really pulling the kids in. We used to have a dozen kids there on a good Sunday and now we average close to forty," agreed Pastor Johnson.

"That's the problem," came the reply over the telephone. "Several weeks ago we made plans with the Schroeders for our two families to take a short vacation trip over this three-day weekend. Now out of a clear blue sky Dave and Mark have announced that either we are back here by 9 o'clock on Sunday morning, or they won't go. It'll ruin all our plans if we have to come back in the middle of the weekend. Pastor, isn't there something you can do?"

"This is the first time in my ministry that I've run into this type problem," replied Pastor Johnson with a laugh, "but I guess I can learn how to cope with it. I'll talk with Mark and Dave this afternoon."

This episode was one of the consequences of the efforts at St. John's to broaden the range of models it used in its Christian education program. Before elaborating on this illustration, however, it may be helpful first to review the variety of educational models that are being used in churches today.

The Teacher-Pupil Model

The most widely used model in Christian education today is one that can best be described as the teacher-pupil model. In this model the teacher is the focal point. This emphasis often is reflected by the placement of the chairs in the rooms—arranged to focus attention on the teacher. This emphasis also may be reflected by a sign on the door proclaiming that this is Mr. Brown's class or Mrs. Jones's class. Typically the responsibility for planning the learning experience and for implementation of these plans rests with the teacher.

For most adults over thirty this is the only educational model they experienced in their youth in elementary school, high school, and Sunday school. It is still widely used in churches and in seminaries, but it is being abandoned by an increasing number of experienced professional educators.

The Curriculum-Centered Model

Perhaps the second most widely used model in the churches today is one in which the curriculum becomes the focal point for the class. This model is over a hundred years old, and part of its popularity goes back to the Uniform Lesson Series, which was introduced in 1872 and which was built around the dream that on any given Sunday every person in every Sunday school would be studying the same passage of Scripture.[1]

During the past quarter century nearly every denomination has introduced two or three "new" curriculum series. In many of these, often to the consternation of those who planned them, the printed materials became the focal point for the class. If one were to judge by appearances, in many parishes there would be only one clear answer to the question "Who is in charge of the church school?" That would be "the curriculum."

The Reconciliation Model

A few years ago one of the fastest-growing models, expecially in adult classes and in vacation church school, was built around the goal of bringing people together in Christian educational experiences across racial lines.

The parallel today is the plan that represents a deliberate attempt to bridge the generation gap. Instead of dividing the membership in the church school along age lines it provides classes that bring together in one group persons from fourteen to ninety years of age.

[1] An excellent book for anyone interested in the evolution of the Sunday school is Robert W. Lynn and Elliott Wright, *The Big Little School* (New York: Harper & Row, 1971).

Both of these are examples of what can be described as the reconciliation model. In this model a heavy emphasis is placed on bringing together for shared educational experiences all kinds of people—across the many boundaries that compartmentalize people in our fragmented society.

In addition to the interracial and intergenerational classes, this model includes groups that bring people together across religious boundaries, ethnic barriers, social-class lines, or geographical divisions such as inner-city–suburban or rural-urban.

The vast majority of these groups meet for a specified period of time with a clearly defined terminal date.

The Event Model

Closely related in several respects to both the curriculum model and the reconciliation model is the event model. It is built around a narrowly defined target with a very brief life. Examples include the "school of religion" sessions held on four Tuesday evenings in the fall, the Bible study group meeting on six Wednesday nights during Lent, the all-day-Saturday field trip, the Sunday evening program with a returned missionary as the featured speaker, or the weekend retreat.

Typically the event stands alone and is not seen as an integral part of a continuing educational experience. The focus usually is on the program or the guest speaker or the subject, and little effort is made to develop meaningful relationships among the participants.

The Experienced-Learning Model

The model that probably is producing the most enthusiastic response from the participants is built around some

152

form of learning by experience. Sometimes called the "action-reflection" model, this approach focuses on the experiences of the participants, rather than on the leader or on printed materials.

Examples of this model include: the adult class that spent a year doing their homework, then took a seventeen-day tour of the Holy Land, and spent the year following the trip reflecting and enlarging on what they had experienced together; the senior-high-school class that writes the curriculum for a different adult class each quarter, whose members take turns "teaching" the adult class that is using their material; the junior-high class that studied worship by attending worship with different congregations on the first and third Sundays of each month, and meeting as a group on the second and fourth Sundays to reflect on these experiences; the intergenerational group that studied the outreach of the church by means of a Saturday field trip once a month and then used this as the subject for that Sunday's "lesson"; the adult class that schedules some form of shared, all-day experiences on the first Sunday of each month and uses this as the subject for shared reflections on the following Sundays; and the class that meets weekly to reflect on the shared experiences of members of the group, using a case-study method.

The Experience Model

In his book *Future Shock* Alvin Toffler asserts that for several decades the economy of the United States was built around the production of goods, but a couple of decades ago the nation moved into an era in which the primary emphasis was on the production of services; and now we are moving into an era when the major emphasis will be on the production of experiences.[2] Coinciding with this has been the emergence of the experience model in Christian education.

Probably the most widely used example of this in recent years has been the record album of the rock opera *Jesus Christ Superstar*. An adult class in a Lutheran parish, which had been averaging sixteen in attendance for years, announced that for the next six weeks they would listen to parts of this record and discuss it. Each of the six Sundays found approximately fifty-four adults present. After six weeks the class returned to its traditional teacher-pupil model—and attendance dropped back to an average of sixteen.

For many people, listening to this album or attending a presentation of the rock opera has been a very meaningful experience. In many parishes this shared experience has been the basis for the introduction of a new but often temporary model in the total Christian education program.

The Inquiry Model

One of the most flexible models being used in the churches goes under several different labels, such as problem-solving, decision-making, discovery- and task-oriented.

In it the members of a class are confronted with a task or a problem or an issue and asked to respond to the challenge by attempting to solve the problem or perform the task or discover the implications of the issue within the frame of reference of a systematic Christian value system. Thus the problem or task or issue—not the study of abstract concepts—becomes the *beginning* point in the

[2] Alvin Toffler, *Future Shock*, (New York: Random House, 1970), pp. 188-242.

learning process. From this specific and easily recognized beginning point the members of the group find themselves forced to construct and defend a value system that enables them to deal with the problem, issue, or task.

The subject matter may vary from a proposal for a building program in the parish to amnesty for young men who went to Canada or Sweden to evade the draft; from providing a public transportation system in the community to financing the local church program; from feeding the starving in Asia to the problems of migrant agricultural laborers; from the proper way to tax farm land to a dress code for high-school students or clergymen.

The Group Model

While not always identified in these terms, the model that often provokes the greatest loyalty to the class among its members and that often has the best attendance-to-membership ratio is the group model. This model was developed in one of the classes at St. John's Church and used to replace the teacher-pupil model for seventh graders.

This model is built in an effort to form groups which will be meaningful to the individual members and to which they can relate on a continuing basis. An example of the group model is the class of women which averages seven in attendance, whose newest member joined the class in 1927 as a newcomer to the community, and which continues to meet in the same room it met in when it was formed in 1923 and had a membership of sixty-five young, single girls. Other examples include the couples' class, which was formed two years ago by a dozen married couples in their mid-twenties, and which meets regularly every Sunday morning, as well as once or twice a month for social and fellowship events; the Tuesday evening Bible study group, which averages nine in attendance out of a membership of ten; the Sunday morning Men's Bible Class, which has met in the same room with the same teacher (and some say, with the same lesson) for twenty-two years; the group that has met every other Monday evening in members' homes, since it was organized two years ago by a dozen people who had shared in a weekend human relations lab; the class of twelve elderly ladies, eleven of them now widowed, that meets in the church parlor every Sunday morning; and the confirmation class that has been meeting with the pastor every Saturday morning for two years.

Why Not Combine Models?

This review of several of the models being used in churches is not offered as a solution for the problems in the church school. It is offered only to help develop a frame of reference in analyzing what is happening in the Christian education program in many parishes.

At St. John's a similar review was undertaken to compare the range of possibilities with the actual program. Everyone, including Pastor Johnson, was surprised to discover that the entire church, despite several efforts at innovation, gradually had drifted toward a heavy dependence on the two models the adult leaders were most familiar with from their own experiences, rather than building from models that children and youth were experiencing in the public schools. As they reflected on this, several of the leaders felt they were moving closer to an understanding of why Sunday school attendance had been declining for several years.

One result of the review was an intentional effort to move in the direction of encouraging the use of several models in one class. This led to the development of the seventh-grade class referred to in the opening paragraphs of this chapter.

A closer examination of this class which had so captured the interest of its members suggests that it was not built solely on the group model. While a major effort was made—and apparently successfully—to build a group that was meaningful to the members (in this case, loyalty to the group is a fringe benefit of the process and not a central goal in itself), this class combined at least two other models in its operation. There was a heavy emphasis on experienced learning and on the use of the inquiry model. The members of the group decided to publish a monthly newspaper that would contain a series of articles interpreting current news events in the light of the teachings of the Old Testament. Thus the basic "curriculum materials" consisted of (1) the Old Testament, (2) current newspapers and newsmagazines, and (3) a corps of six enthusiastic and imaginative, enabler type adults who work with the group.

It is important to offer people a wider range of choices than has been the tradition in most congregations. As people become increasingly accustomed to being given a choice in nearly every other segment of life, a rapidly growing number are expecting the churches to be more flexible.

Offering people a choice of models in the church school is also a means of preventing other problems from arising.

Building in both a range of choices and a combination

of two or three models in each class can reduce the chances of the members' turning the class into an inward-looking clique that restricts the horizons of the members and excludes strangers by the invisible wall it builds around itself.

Another example of the value of building in more diversity is illustrated by a statement made to Pastor Johnson after he arrived at St. John's. A thirty-year-old Sunday school teacher said to him, with fire in her eye and conviction in her voice, "Here at St. John's most of the church school teachers are cowards. The teachers of the classes for children and youth are drawn almost entirely from people who are afraid to go to adult classes. All five of our adult classes are taught by authoritarian personalities who won't tolerate any free discussion or open debate or disagreement with their views!"

As he smiled at this comment, Pastor Johnson knew he had another ally.

16

Sunday's Eggs and
the Women's Organization

What do "Sunday's eggs," the decline of the women's organization in many congregations, and the importance of ownership of goals have in common?

Six or seven decades ago, when rural churches constituted a large share of the strength of American Protestantism, the foreign missionary movement was either the child or the parent of the women's organization in thousands of congregations in several denominations. In many rural churches the women accepted most or all of the congregation's responsibility for financing the work of foreign missionaries. One of the many methods of raising money the women in rural churches used was to designate for missions the money received from the sale of the eggs the chickens laid on Sunday.

Some of the more zealous of these supporters of the missionary enterprise would gather the eggs at noon on Saturday, ostensibly because of the Saturday afternoon trip to town, when the eggs would be traded at the general store for groceries needed for the coming week. Perhaps because of company's coming over on Sunday afternoon or a trip to visit relatives, the farmer's wife would "forget" to gather the eggs on Sunday evening and might not remember this chore until sometime Monday morning. As a result her chickens often had 44 to 48 hours to work for the Lord every Sunday.

While it may be true, as some cynics have charged, that for a few women this was a subtle form of one-upmanship to publicize the productivity of their flocks, most of the women extended the working hours of their hens every Sunday because they knew that Brother Ben over in Africa and Miss Mary in India were dependent on those Sunday eggs for the financial support of their work.

There are at least three reasons for recounting this story here. The first is, at least one-half the pastors of congregations that are more than forty years old are hearing statements like these from older women in the congregation.

"The young women just don't seem to be interested in our organization anymore."

"We used to have twelve circles, now we don't have enough interested women to form six circles."

"The only reason I agreed to be president of our women's organization next year is that the nominating committee came to me and said they felt the only chance we had to reach the younger women was to pick a younger person to be president—but I'm fifty-eight."

"It doesn't matter what we plan for the monthly program, we always have the same old faces. Last Thursday, as I drove to church, I was thinking about this. I guessed we would have fifteen women at the meeting, and I began to list them in my head. I was right on the number, even though one person I expected to be there was sick. Her place was taken by a lady who attends once or twice a year and happened to come last week."

In literally thousands of local Protestant churches the women's organization ranked with the Sunday school as one of the two strongest organizations in the congregation. In at least one third of these same congregations what once was a strong and vital organization appears to be dying. Why? In perhaps another fourth, or even a third it is far weaker than it was a few decades ago. Why?

In many parishes the women's organization was an exceptionally effective organization. It was successful in assimilating into the fellowship of the church the young bride from another community who married a young man from the neighborhood. It was also very effective in welcoming the wife of the couple who had just moved into the neighborhood, in initiating into the ranks of womanhood the person who had been a giggly teen-ager only a few years earlier, and in serving as an extremely valuable support group for the woman who had suddenly lost her husband. Today's young women do not appear interested in becoming a part of this organization. Why?

While some people will dispute this, the women's organization may have been the most effective educational organization in the history of American Protestantism. It studied subject matter that included not only the Bible, but also foreign affairs, race relations, Christian social action, world geography, folklore, international relations, languages, and parliamentary procedure. Today in many congregations the focus is either on (a) fellowship and money-raising or (b) money-raising and fellowship. Why does the carefully planned program that would have attracted a crowd of two hundred in 1939 now produce an attendance of only forty out of a congregation that is twice as large as it was back in 1939?

Many different reasons are being offered to explain the

decline of the women's organization. These range from television to the tremendous increase in the number of women employed outside the home and the growing competition for people's discretionary time.

While there are undoubtedly many reasons for this widespread trend in the parish women's organization, the thesis of this chapter is that the most important single reason can be found in the story of "Sunday's eggs."

To put it in more positive terms, the major reason the women's organization in the local church thrived during the first several decades of this century was that it had a clearly defined, easily understood, biblically sound, and psychologically viable reason for being. It had a purpose. This purpose was outreach and service to others. The organization drew on the basic teachings of the Christian faith and the neighbor-centered concern of the individual Christian woman in the fulfillment of that purpose.

In those congregations where the central purpose of the women's organization was the support of the foreign (and later, national) missionary enterprise, the purpose was not only clearly defined, but also expressed in goals that were fully understood and completely "owned" by the women in the parishes. The farmer's wife who gave her hens a few extra hours to lay eggs to help finance a missionary's work in Africa was not primarily concerned with raising money. Her primary concern was the furtherance of a cause in which she felt a real sense of ownership.

Such highly visible dimensions of the local women's organization as the opportunities for fellowship, assimilation of newcomers into the fellowship, money-raising activities and events, interest in Christian social action, and educational programs were either means to an end or "fringe benefits." They were not ends in themselves.

During the past quarter century three developments have contributed to the weakening of the women's organizations in the local church. One which has been a pattern in several denominations is the shifting of responsibility for the implementation of the entire foreign and home missionary enterprise from the women's organization to the general church. In some denominations in years past the women "owned" the whole program and carried almost the complete financial responsibility for the work. In others the women owned a clearly identified share of the foreign and home missionary efforts of the denomination and carried the complete responsibility for financing their own piece of the action. In recent years, however, the trend has been to "realign" or "restructure" or "reorganize" to encourage the women to see themselves as an integral part of a wholistic approach to mission and ministry. An inevitable and predictable result has been to dilute the definition of purpose for the local women's organization.

A second development has been that with the passage of time, and with the increase in sensitivity to the needs of people (see pages 106-7 for an elaboration of this point), the growing interest in the social problems at home, the decline in the spirit of imperialism in the United States, and the rise of nationalism in Asia, Africa, and South America since 1945, the churches' interest, involvement, and investment in the foreign missionary enterprise does not loom as large in the definition of outreach today as it did in 1939 or 1948 or 1953. Their distinctive purpose has been diluted by their involvement with a long list of other concerns.

The third development of this era, and the second reason for recounting this story of Sunday eggs, is that the women's organization in the parish, like every other organization created by human beings, has become vulnerable to a very common form of institutional blight: the gradual transformation of the means to an end into an end in itself. The raising of money, the monthly educational programs, the mission study groups, and the visits from returned missionaries were more important and more attractive when they were but a means for fulfilling a clearly defined purpose. The fellowship opportunities, the broad base of participation, and the assimilation of newcomers were very important fringe benefits, but, like so many fringe benefits, they can be achieved most effectively when they are not reached for directly, but are realized as a dividend from some other effort or activity.

What does all of this say to the pastor and people who are actively concerned about the purpose, role, and future of the women's organization in the parish?

First, a bleak future awaits any local women's organization in which the major emphasis is on fellowship, study groups, and money-raising ventures.

Second, relatively few younger women, whether they are employed outside the home or not, will be attracted by an organization that has allowed the means to an end to become the end itself.

Third, those local women's organizations that have defined or redefined a purpose for themselves built around outreach, neighbor-centered concerns, and the imperative to witness to the gospel are vigorous and vital organizations today. There are many of these, their purposes covering a wide and varied range of concerns; and their number appears to be growing.

Finally, and here is the third reason for telling the story of Sunday's eggs, it is absolutely vital that each woman in the local church feel the same kind of attachment to or ownership of the purpose and goals of her organization that the farmer's wife felt when she was motivated to arrange a forty-hour Sunday for her hens. How that can be done in today's complex society is relevant to all expressions of ministry in and through the church and therefore merits a separate chapter.

17

Yours or Mine?

The recent emphasis in churches on goals, goal-setting procedures, and management by objective (MBO) has produced at least two highly visible results. One is widespread confusion over the definition and proper use of such terms as *purpose, goal,* and *objective.*

The other is a reasonably clear operational distinction between a "good" goal or objective and a "bad" one. This distinction comes through very clearly in even the briefest evaluation of the goal-setting efforts of the federal government, national agencies of the various denominations, special citizens' committees on metropolitan problems, regional judicatories of the various denominations, upper-middle-class parents concerned about the careers of their children, individual congregations, whites who are greatly concerned about race relations and who develop a set of goals for blacks, and outgoing organizational officers who feel obligated to define the goals their successors should implement.

In each case it has turned out that in operational terms a good goal was one in which the persons responsible for implementing it and living with the consequences of it were involved in formulating it. A bad goal was one in which the persons responsible for implementing it were not involved in its formulating.

One of the points of "discontinuity" in our society, to borrow a term from the brilliant economist and Episcopalian Peter Drucker,[1] is that the majority of adults in the United States grew up in a culture where it was an acceptable and reasonably effective procedure for one group of people to formulate goals that would be assigned to another group of people. Unfortunately for the peace of mind and the emotional tranquillity of thousands of adult authoritarian leaders, would-be leaders, husbands, fathers, new town planners, presbyterians, pastors, white leaders in race relations, foremen, teachers, and presidents of organizations, this concept has been officially demolished as a workable operational procedure by the late Douglas McGregor and a host of his colleagues and disciples.[2] If he were alive Dr. McGregor probably would object to credit being given him here and point out that in his proposal to replace the theory X of motivation with his theory Y he was simply articulating facts that many people already knew intuitively about the world as it really is today.

This brings up one of the most important contributions that people in a congregation have a right to expect of their pastor in today's world. As one of the leaders of the congregation, as an authority on the Christian doctrine of man, as a consultant to his own congregation on the process of defining mission and formulating goals, and as a partner with his people in God's work, the pastor

[1] Peter Drucker, *The Age of Discontinuity* (New York: Harper & Row, 1969).

[2] Douglas McGregor, *The Human Side of Enterprise* (New York: McGraw-Hill Book Co., 1960), pp. 33-57.

is expected, and rightly so, to help the people develop a broad ownership base for any goals that are articulated by or for that parish. The people in the congregation also have an obligation to remember that their pastor is a human being, a sinner, and cannot be an expert in everything. Therefore, he too is certain to make mistakes.

How can a congregation develop a broad base of ownership in the goals it sets for itself?

The traditional approach has been for the governing body of the congregation—the session, the official board, the vestry, or the church council—to formulate and adopt a set of goals. Since they are the duly elected and properly authorized representatives of the congregation, the other members can be expected to fall in behind their leadership and to assist in the efforts to implement these goals and objectives.

The most serious limitation on this approach today is that in an increasing number of congregations it does not work. (Persons who have high blood pressure or weak hearts or who are firmly committed to a presbyterian church polity may find it wise to skip the rest of this chapter. Much of what follows is clearly heresy if measured by traditional standards of representative government, presbyterian polity, or connectionalism.)

In churches with a congregational church polity it has become increasingly popular for a properly elected, goal-setting committee to submit its list of suggested or recommended goals to be reviewed and adopted at a congregational meeting. This system does help establish a stronger sense of ownership among those who were on the prevailing side in every vote. However, in many cases most of these people already had a strong sense of ownership in the suggested goals, since perhaps twelve of the typical twenty-three people who bothered to come to that congregational meeting would have been members or spouses of members of the committee that formulated the recommended goals. This process does little for those—usually a majority of the membership—who stayed away, and it rarely increases the sense of ownership among those on the losing side when the votes were cast.

A third approach was developed by a church in Osceola, Indiana, and has been used by many others. The process began when the leaders of this six-hundred-member congregation asked all the members to suggest programs, activities, events, and ministries they believed their church should be involved in during the coming year.

Next these were collated to eliminate duplications, resulting in a list of perhaps sixty to one hundred different ideas and suggestions.

Each member was then asked to sign up for the one program—or two or three or four—that he would like to help plan in detail and to share in implementing.

The "contract" between the church and the membership is that the congregation will undertake only those programs and ministries that have the support of an adequate number of members. If no one signs up to help plan and implement a program or ministry, even though it appears to be a "good idea," it is not begun.

Several other churches have used the same basic procedure, but utilize two refinements. After the suggestions for programs, activities, events, and ministries have been collated, a group of experienced persons work through the list and add one or two sets of numbers in parentheses after each suggestion. The first number is calculated for every suggestion and represents the estimated number of persons that will be needed to plan and implement that program or activity. Unless that number of signatures is reached, that item is scratched from the list.

One result of this may be the spontaneous creation of a series of independent *ad hoc* "priority committees" or "promotional groups" or inspired "salesmen." Many of those who offered suggestions they believed to be of crucial importance and top priority begin to "sell" friends and acquaintances on their plans. The important ministry or program that is represented by item number 39 on the list requires seven signers if it is to be implemented, "so I certainly hope you'll sign up for number 39 if you possibly can, for with your help we can make that one go!"

Before jumping to a conclusion as to whether that kind of "lobbying" in a congregation is good or bad, (a) compare that picture with the way "volunteers" are recruited in your parish and (b) use the concept of a cost-benefit formula in making your own evaluation.

The other refinement is the adding of a second number to those suggestions where it is appropriate to do so. This second number refers to the estimated number of additional dollars that will be required to implement this proposed program. In one church, for example, a proposal was made to have a free luncheon one Sunday a month for anyone who wanted to come. While it would be directed at the many lonesome, elderly persons who live within a few blocks of this congregation's meeting place, anyone would be welcome. The idea was copied from another parish that had been doing this and could furnish an experience record for guidance in calculating costs. When this proposal was referred back to the membership it was followed by two numbers in parentheses, (8) and ($900). These meant that it would not be adopted and implement unless (a) at least eight people volunteered to give one day a month in time and (b) an additional $900 a year was pledged to the church budget. In other words, the terms of the contract were clear on both the proposed program addition and the anticipated costs.

Incidentally, the typical pattern in those churches using this system is to operate on a fiscal year that coincides with the calendar year and a program year that coincides with the school year. This means that the program planning is usually done in the spring and early summer. Thus it is relatively easy for members to understand why any new program proposals will require additional financing beyond the pledges made the previous fall to the regular church budget which includes a "unified" appeal for both the basic operating expenses of the congregation such as utilities, staff salaries, insurance, pension obligations and also the regular denominational askings for benevolences.

Enough experience has been accumulated by congregations using this system to broaden the base of ownership of programmatic goals that it is possible to see some of the pitfalls and objections that may be ahead of the congregation that is considering it for the first time.

The most serious pitfall appears to be in communications. It is somewhere between difficult and impossible to introduce this system into a congregation by mail. A simple unified budget appeal probably is best for the congregation that depends on the mails rather than on face-to-face contacts. The suggestions for programs, activities, events, and ministries can be gathered most effectively by face-to-face contacts. These may be made through every member visitation programs, a series of small group meetings in homes, two or three large covered-dish dinners at the church, telephone calls, or some other method. The best results tend to follow when the system includes at least two different procedures for enabling each member to feed his suggestions into the process.

The system also is more effective when each person is contacted on a face-to-face basis during round two of the process when members are asked to choose where they would like to be involved. When this is done by mail the sign-up rate tends to drop so sharply that it begins to nullify the central objective of broadening the base of ownership of goals and program.

A second pitfall is that some people who have been trained in a system that emphasizes representative church government have great difficulty in conceptualizing this new process. Instead of seeing this as an opportunity to broaden the participation base in the congregation, they see it as a careless abandoning of carefully nurtured procedures and traditions and as an opening of the door to a chaotic, thoughtless, and irresponsible form of decision-making. They see the whole procedure as being based on what they perceive as a fallacious notion, the idea that it is good to encourage everyone to "do his own thing."

When comments such as these are voiced by two or three of the most influential leaders, it probably means that the congregation is faced with two common and very basic issues. The first comes under the label of institutional blight. It surfaces when the means to an end become ends in themselves. (At this point someone may quote the sentence alleged to be the last seven words of the church: "We never did it that way before!")

The other issue is what this chapter is all about: What are the goals of this congregation and who owns them? In other words, whenever a new idea is introduced into an organization and a potential veto group feels no sense of ownership in that new idea, the normal, natural, and human initial response is to exercise the veto.[3]

When this second pitfall is anticipated, the appropriate procedure may be to postpone the issue of ownership of the *content* of goals until later and to focus first on the issue of ownership of the *procedures* to be used in formulating goals.

In addition to these two pitfalls—which can sabotage the whole system—the introduction and application of this approach to goal-setting tend to produce three objections that can be handled more effectively when they have been anticipated.

The first objection usually comes from a few persons who have been active leaders in the congregation for many years. With their long experience and overall grasp of the total picture of the life and program of that parish, they are naturally inclined to believe that they know best where Mrs. Jones's skills and Bill White's talents can be utilized most efficiently. This procedure not only allows, but positively encourages Mrs. Jones, Bill White, and all the others to choose their own areas of service rather than accept an assignment, made by knowledgeable leaders, to a position where their talents are most urgently needed. How long will it take for the whole parish to fall apart if everyone is allowed to pick his own job without regard *to* filling the key positions with the best qualified persons?

This raises a basic philosophical question. Is it possible and desirable today to manage people in the same style that has prevailed for decades?

The second objection is heard most commonly in congregations which have a presbyterian polity. "This whole

[3] For other comments on the veto power see Schaller, *Parish Planning,* pp. 75-86.

idea is simply incompatible with our traditional presbyterian form of church government" is one of the basic expressions of this objection. The objectors are absolutely correct. This system for broadening the base of ownership of the goals of the church runs counter to traditional presbyterian polity.

One way to respond to this objection is to use the cost-benefit form of analysis in weighing the arguments. In some congregations the weight of argument may be on the side of continuing traditional practices; in another, the anticipated benefits from broadening the participation base may be seen as more than offsetting the costs. Purists on presbyterian polity, however, may have difficulties with this pragmatic test of the value of tradition.

The third objection to this procedure revolves around the concept of "designated giving.' Opponents of designated giving contend that for the church to encourage members to earmark their financial contributions will lead to an underfinancing of the unglamorous but necessary functions, while the more highly visible and attractive programs will be dividing up a disproportionately large share of the church's income.

This may be a valid point, but it tends to conceal the basic issue under the surface of supporting or opposing designated giving. The basic question is not whether designated giving is good or bad, but rather who is going to do the designating and how does a local church function in a society in which designated giving is an accepted fact of life.

The process of designated giving begins when the church member receives his paycheck. In one way or another he designates how much of his income he is going to contribute to the many appeals that are directed at him from charitable, religious, educational, political, and philanthropic causes. These may include the Boy Scouts, the United Fund, his church, a political organization, a children's home, the building fund for a new Y building, his service club, and the private college his son wants to attend.

One of the probable reasons that the increase in total giving to all such causes has been greater during the past decade than the increase in giving to religious organizations is that the quantity and quality of the competition for the church member's tithe is greater today than it was in 1955 or 1960.

One approach to this problem has been for churches to ask for special gifts for special projects that have visibility and attractiveness.

This is not a new development. This pattern goes back into centuries of history. The traditional response of churches has been to encourage their members to continue their regular level of giving for the general work of the church and to supplement it with special, earmarked, second-mile giving. This procedure has been used in both individual congregations and denominations. It has been used for missions, education, building programs, and a host of special projects.

The emphasis given the concept of a unified budget during the past quarter century has tended to discourage the use of supplemental or second-mile or special, designated giving in favor of one budget which includes all funds and programs. The approach suggested here is a "both-and" system which conserves the values of the unified budget *and* also systematically opens the door to *additional* designated giving. This recognizes the realities of today's world. An essential element of the traditional unified budget system is that somewhere in the process some person or group must designate how many dollars go to which needs. Since the total dollar requests usually exceed the number of dollars available this becomes a win-lose game, and there is great competition for the power that goes with the position of designating the winners and losers. Thus today's argument about designated giving is actually a facade over the real issue. This is the location of the power to choose the winners and losers.[4]

All three of these objections can be responded to more effectively if they are discussed in the larger context of participatory democracy. When is it best to delegate responsibility for making decisions to others and when is it best to broaden the base of participation?

Robert A. Dahl offers a frame of reference for looking at this issue and identifies three important criteria in making this choice as (1) the degree to which the decisions made by others are in accord with my value system; (2) the place for specialized skill, competence, or knowledge; and (3) the economy of time, attention, and energy.[5] This set of criteria is also useful to the pastor and the people in the parish when they discuss how the ownership of goals can be shared so that fewer will look at the goals and programs of the church and identify them as "theirs," and more will respond to them as "ours."

[4] While many behavioral scientists advocate eliminating the win/lose concept in discussing the development of the ideal organization, every political system is by definition operated as a distributive system. If the parish or a denomination is viewed as a distributive system which is involved in the allocation of scarce resources (money, manpower, time, talent, energy, etc.) there will be winners and losers. For a useful discussion of this point see William B. Eddy and Robert J. Saunders, "Applied Behavioral Science in Urban Administrative Political Systems," *Public Administration Review*, January-February 1972, pp. 11-16.

[5] Robert A. Dahl, *After the Revolution?* (New Haven: Yale University Press, 1970), pp. 3-58.